Acknowledgments

My greatest debt of gratitude is to the thousands of children whose unquestioning participation in the projects I have planned have enabled me to develop my ideas as a teacher and organiser of literature projects. For 35 years I have enjoyed sharing the other worlds of literature with primary children whose enthusiasm and diverse ways of responding have always delighted me. I particularly acknowledge the children in the five schools where I spent most of my teaching career: Higher Bebington County Junior School, Woodlands County Junior School, Tarvin County Primary School, Redhills Combined School and Taliesin Junior School.

Thanks are also due to the children and teachers involved in the many literature-based projects which I organised as arts in schools coordinator in Clwyd in the late 1980s and early 1990s. For their generous and enthusiastic support of my work I wish to thank Keith Evans, former director of education in Clwyd and Keith McDonogh, director of education for Flintshire.

There are also certain key educationists whose ideas and advice have shaped my thinking. They are Vernon Hale, former primary advisor for Cheshire, Malcolm Ross, former reader in arts education at the University of Exeter, Christopher Parry, formerly of the University of Wales, who supervised my doctorate, and Rex Gibson of the Shakespeare and Schools Project.

I wish to thank my own four children, Dunstan, Imogen, Lawrence and Beatrice, whose responses to stories, books and the life around them have taught me more than any education books I have read.

Finally, to all the storytellers I have heard and all the stories which have entered my memory, acknowledgments are due. These ought to be detailed and specific, but cannot be because I do not remember them that way!

Contents

Chapter One

Reading the other worlds of fiction

'My lord', said Pwyll, 'good day to you.
From what country do you come?'
'From the Other World', he replied.
'I am Arawn, King of the Other World'.[1]

Literacy and playing

The National Literacy Strategy can be viewed as the latest in a series of victories for those who routinely mock the 'child-centred' approach to primary education. So self-confident have these forces become that they respond to all alternative arguments with equal contempt. So it was that in the early summer of 1999 the Secretary of State, Mr Blunkett, dismissed criticism of the Strategy as 'blatant elitism dressed up as well-intentioned liberalism'. Those who believed in putting children at the centre of their own education were characterised as those taking for granted 'the failure of half of our pupils'.[2]

Yet the unease among parents, teachers, children and others after more than a year of the Strategy is growing and the arguments cannot be so easily dismissed. Many children are bored, their teachers burdened with too much tedious planning, their parents anxious about their children's waning levels of interest. Although this might be an over-simplification, there are too many examples for the discomfort to be shrugged off. As the Strategy is allied to tests, targets and excessive prescriptions for such things as homework, there appears to be a threat to children's opportunities to play both at school and at home.

The threat to play must be taken seriously. The word 'play', more than any other, is associated with the 'child-centred' approach but we restrict play at our peril. Play is as important to the development of children who are healthy in body, mind and spirit as ever it was. As Patrick Bateson argues:

> Children are not miniature adults. Some of their behaviour is like scaffolding – a specialised structure used in the process of building the adult, which loses its use once this task is completed. Play is an important example of such developmental scaffolding, and without it the adult is more difficult to build.[3]

The kinds of play relevant when we consider literacy are all those concerned with the imagination, role-play, play with language, visual play, the development of a creativity in handling words, ideas and feelings.

In this book I am seeking common ground between two apparently opposite positions. In Chapters 4, 5 and 6, for instance, I present a comprehensive range of lessons which fully realise appropriate learning objectives in the literacy strategy. But they do so within a context of creative, playful endeavour in which dance, drama and the arts play their full part. First, however, it is important to consider the natural, playful relationship that often exists between the child and the book before the child goes to school.

Wefts of meaning

Little Beatrice, 15 months old, sits on the lounge carpet with a book. She runs her finger along the lines of words, making a high-pitched 'oi-ee-oi-ee-oi-ee' sound. Undoubtedly, she is reading in one sense of the word. Perhaps 'para-reading' would be more precise a definition. She does this often on car journeys too, babbles away happily with her Postman Pat or her Squirrel Nutkin. Her brother, Lawrie, four years old, used to put his teddy on his knee and do the same thing, in this case reading to someone else! They are playing and they are reading, but they are not playing in the same way as when they offer to make a cup of tea in a toy cup. There is a difference. Beatrice says 'pretend' in this latter situation, because it is a social occasion involving someone else in the game. Her para-reading is not so self aware. She is talking the book into life, even though the words are formed of wordless sounds. She is imitating the behaviour of many adults in her life.

Next, however, Beatrice climbs onto her father's knee. He is wearing a loosely woven sweater. She looks at this weave and is attracted to its horizontals, the wefts. She runs her finger along these wefts and makes the same high pitched sounds. This time she is reading to her father from the 'book' of the sweater. It is different. It is 'pretend'. She has switched her playing mode and made an exciting link, seeing how things in the world have coherence. In a sense she has made a metaphor, an equation, has perceived a harmony within a game, sitting in a reading context and playing with one of the most powerful symbols of education and influence in society. She is relating life with text, text with life, seeing the links between patterns in her home.

If such wefts are lines of meaning in literature, then the warps are the lines of meaning in life for the child and the real significance of literature can only be felt if a weave is made. Literature, as opposed to oral language, can remain outside of life because it is in objects which can remain untouched on a shelf. Oral language is instant, living communication, whereas literature has to be brought out of its hiding place. That is why so many people down the ages have had far greater difficulty learning to read and write than learning to listen and talk. So, literature relies heavily on readers to make very deliberate efforts to help non-reading children make the weave successfully. Readers can do this in three simple ways: by reading in the presence of children; by telling and reading stories and poems to them; and by sharing the reading experience. They will often fail in their efforts to give this help if they only concentrate on the wefts themselves without relating them to the warps, life itself. Among the warps there are those which are personal to each individual and those which are part of the shared world. People who seek to help others to become readers may fail in their attempts if they focus solely on the warps which are external and ignore the personal, the unique, the peculiar.

Consider the two worlds in the literary experiences of Lawrie, a year earlier. After his mother finishes reading one of Alison Uttley's *Little Fox Stories*[4] he is powerfully moved. He bursts out, 'I'd like to get into that book and run through the wood and smash the glass cage and let the little unicorn's daddy out!' A little later he is getting used to the medium of the book, its objectness, it as an external form, relating this knowledge to a desired external phenomenon and saying to his brother, 'Hey Dunny, can I have a chapter of tickling?' Literature and life, life and literature are making one fabric.

Like most young children Lawrie is also revealing how much more alive to his context he is than most adults. Children constantly notice things and make fresh relationships, or equations. These things are maybe trivial to adults, but children will notice and connect them – objects or patterns, symbols or codes – it doesn't seem to matter. The process is powerful, almost unstoppable, and is marked by the making of metaphorical equations between the unfamiliar and the familiar. It is a vital component of learning for children.

So the code of a book itself can have the same domestic significance as the sweater's weave or the mesh in a fireguard. It is quite clear, too, that the object known as 'book' can take its place alongside pan, chair, table, Duplo or teddy. Such domestic objects are key factors in a baby's construction of objective reality. Certain objects, however, have a special kind of significance, satisfying the baby's need in what D. W. Winnicott calls the 'intermediate area'. This, claims Winnicott, lies between the baby's absolute identification with the mother and objective reality. It occurs towards the end of the baby's first year. This 'intermediate area' or 'potential space' is where play and cultural experience are located and 'it depends for its existence on living experiences, not on inherited tendencies'.[5]

Winnicott claims that 'playing has a place and time' and that when children play they exercise a form of 'magical control' over the world outside. So, when Beatrice 'reads' her father's sweater she exercises 'magical control' in that her magic turns the sweater into a book. At eighteen months she is skilled in operating 'magical control' over everyday objects and such play is no trivial matter. According to Winnicott it is of utmost seriousness, this coming together of genetic self with outside reality.[6]

There is a time when a baby first ventures into this 'intermediate area'. This is often manifested in a clinging to particular objects or, maybe, one object. Winnicott calls these special objects 'transitional objects' and the play is directed towards them (teddies or bits of soft blankets with names). They represent for the baby the 'transition from a state of being merged with the mother to a state of being in relation to the mother as something outside and separate'. A typical encounter between baby and object would be recognisable by the lifting and moving about of the object by the baby into a range of different positions, accompanied by the articulation of actual or made-up words, often in a constant stream.[7]

This time in a child's life, coveted by the toy industry, has vital implications for the development of imagination. It is the beginning of something which will affect a person's whole life. Winnicott is fully aware of its significance: 'This intermediate area of experience . . . constitutes the greater part of the infant's experience, and throughout life is retained in the intense experiencing that belongs to the arts and to religion and to imaginative living, and to creative scientific work.[8]

To the infant the object is of massive importance while it lasts as a 'transitional object' but the thing itself is not 'transitional'. It is the infant's behaviour, the playing just away from the mother figure, just short of independence, which is 'transitional'. So, during this fascinating time, the object will be obsessively desired. It is a symbol of security, an object of passions, including intense hatred as well as love. Intrinsically, however, it may have no value at all.

For several years I wondered about the possible place of the book in this scheme of objects surrounding the growing baby. At one time I even considered that books, perhaps, could perform the transitional role, particularly the rag, puffy plastic and doll kind of books. Maybe they could, but not as books. The particular significance of books would be absent from the role as 'transitional object'. It would be interesting to know what Dr Winnicott's view on this would have been.

Perhaps, though, it is unimportant. Although this 'intermediate area of experience . . . constitutes the greater part of the infant's experience' the 'transitional object' itself dies for the child. It is, therefore, a temporary focus for an experiential need that moves on to other objects. Winnicott puts it in this perspective: 'It loses meaning . . . because the transitional phenomena have become *diffused* . . . spread out over the whole intermediate territory between 'inner . . . reality' and 'the external world', . . . that is to say, over the whole cultural field'.[9]

So the need is there for ever after the death of the importance of the teddy or the piece of rag trailing from the hand, thumb in mouth. At the moment of *diffusion*, what might be there to take the place of the 'transitional object'? Domestic objects will teem into that space and the baby will imitate other people's behaviour in relation to them. That is why the quality of other people's models of behaviour is so important.

This moment of diffusion in the 'intermediate area' or 'potential space' between mother and outside world is one of the more important times in an individual's life. This is when the book, which might have been merely lying around or, hopefully, in the hand of the baby's parents and siblings, can come into its own. This will not be as a transitional phenomenon but as a signpost and symbol for a new set of relationships in 'the whole cultural field'.

The uniqueness of a book at this moment lies in its duality as an object. At one and the same time it is a physical object in the immediate hinterland of the baby's life and it is a transporter of all kinds of subjective references. Not only is it an object in the 'real world', like a table, saucepan or squeaking ball, but it is also a conveyor of the same kinds of *magic* which have been conjured in stories, songs and rhymes by the tongues of parents and others.

During his tenth month of life we bought Lawrie his first book, a stuffed plastic version of *Spot's Friends*[10] with bright pictures and a delicious chewy surface! On the way home in the buggy he became fractious, so out came the book as a pacifier. As soon as he got it in his hands he tore off the paper in great excitement and buried his face in it, rubbing and sniffing with ecstasy. He was literally 'burying his head in a book'! Soon other books joined it and certain ones held sway for long periods.

Lawrence babyhandled his books in much the same way that he treated most objects, but quickly discovered the secret that makes a book different. To his senses it must have seemed something like this : slices which you can flick over and when you do so everything changes. New shapes, new colours, new sounds and stories from Mummy's or Daddy's lips, a whole new game. Some of his books were designed to exploit just this sense of change from page to page or slice to slice. John S. Goodall's *Creepy Castle*[11], for instance, has half pages which make one picture lead directly into the next as a transformation. Books such as Dick Bruna's *Animal Book*[12] helped to emphasise to Lawrence the links between the book and the physical world. It held a potential for a form of dance in which animal movements could be simulated with hands and their sounds imitated with the voice. Links with everyday reality were cemented also for Lawrence in so many of the pictures in his early books. The waving figure, an incidental in Pienkowski's *Shapes*[13], drew a 'bye-bye' from him, and the mermaid combing her long blonde hair in the same book made him comb his with his fingers. Books were pouring into the intermediate area for him.

The objects and books that children use and play with are to them tokens of the culture which surrounds them. Each child will embrace a unique selection and will evolve into the culture in an individualistic way. Such tokens are cultural objects and the nature of the child's selection will affect his or her cultural growth to a greater or lesser degree. The book is universally acknowledged as one of the most important tokens in our culture and its place must be secured at this vital time, the first three years, alongside all the other objects in the child world.

The National Literacy Strategy

Beyond this time of life, and particularly when they go to school, many children experience debilitating problems concerning the understanding of the code of a book. Nowhere has the educational debate been more hotly fought than in the best ways of solving this problem. The current solution, embodied in the National Literacy Strategy, consolidates the victory of analysis over synthesis, of those advocating behaviourist strategies over supporters of the so-called 'real books' approach. Buoyed by a landslide majority and eager to fulfil its leader's battle cry of 'Education, education, education', the New Labour government saw targets and strategies as the way forward.

The 'Framework for teaching' is in favour of a cognitive approach in which children learn a range of strategies, called 'searchlights', to 'get at the meaning of a text'.[14] The strategy – along with a similar one for numeracy – is geared 'to raising standards as high as possible'. Although nobody in their right mind would contest such an aim, the criteria for judging these standards is open to challenge. They are crude: 'in 2002, 80% of 11-year-olds are expected to reach level 4 or above in the Key Stage 2 English tests'.[15] Setting aside the dubious nature and conduct of the tests themselves, this is hardly a convincing way of establishing the reading and writing health of the nation. It is, however, the logical conclusion of a process which began more than twenty-five years before in the rise of behaviour modification techniques in the United States, in which only that which is objectively measurable is used to make judgments and determine policies.

The development of the National Literacy Strategy out of demands by powerful figures such as HMCI Chris Woodhead has been marked by a lack of well-planned and targeted research. This is hardly surprising, as Mr Woodhead consistently expresses contempt for universities and colleges and their educational research findings. Consequently, the Strategy and its Framework are based more on assertion than proof, more on random examples of good practice than consistently tested hypotheses. As with all behaviour modification projects in education, it is the cognitive aspect of children's behaviour rather than the affective which matters. Instead of viewing reading as a process of a lifetime which begins with early playing experiences, this approach deals with reading and writing in terms of targets, objectives, scores and levels.

Learning to read, for successful children, however, is more like gradual changes being made to a familiar room so that it always remains familiar, even though it may one day be very different from the room of years before. The best books to begin this long process are those familiar ones with their well-known patterns. Just as a baby builds an intimacy with domestic objects, the infant can build intimacy with letter, word and phrase in the wefts of his books. Frank Smith is certain of this: '. . . visually there is nothing in reading that the eyes and brain do not accomplish when we look around a room to locate an object or to distinguish one face from another.'[16]

Smith claims that anyone who can 'distinguish a pin from a paper clip' should find learning to read easy. If one considers the thousands of objects known and differentiated by most children at five years of age, from parts of their own bodies to gadgets, tools, toys and things in the garden, it is a wonder any of them have problems with learning to read. Perhaps part of the explanation is that we educators can teach children not to want to read. Attitudes, choice of material, systems, methods and the sheer pressure placed upon the school's role in teaching children to read seem often to have the opposite effect: 'A child may learn not to want to read, or not to expect to be able to read, or may even learn to approach reading in ways that will have the effect of always making it difficult or impossible.'[17]

A close scrutiny of 'The Termly Objectives' listed in the Framework suggests that the National Literacy Strategy may add to this problem rather than solving it. The Framework is a behaviourist's paradise, resembling the plans for the complex circuitry involved in an electricity substation! Small wonder so many teachers are unnerved by it and so many children bored by it. In such circumstances teachers are bound to play safe, to attempt to fulfil the lists of objectives without seeing the broader picture. Early soundings have confirmed that the strategy is off target, despite causing a fever of activity throughout the system in which hard-pressed head teachers and English coordinators sit in meetings with local education authority officers setting targets which are often plucked out of the air. Such targets more often pay little or no attention to the children involved. It is the eight out of ten, the 80 per cent, rather than the Gemmas and Jameses that matter.

Living in other worlds

One of the inducements to reading once offered to children was that this set of skills could gain you entrance into 'other worlds of the imagination'. This sage expression has a convincing truth which is just as relevant in the age of television and the internet as it was in the age of the epic novel. This great inducement was usually elaborated:

through reading you could travel into the age of the Romans or journey to the other side of the world; through reading you could walk beside Odysseus or share the problems of Oliver Twist!

If this is true, being unable to read amounts to a devastating form of exclusion. No wonder those who cannot read suffer a sense of alienation. The struggling reader resembles the lame boy in Browning's 'The Pied Piper of Hamelin' who cannot follow the other children into the other world, and *this* 'other world' is tantalisingly close to the everyday world:

> For he led us, he said, to a joyous land
> Joining the town and *just at hand* . . .

This 'lost' world is a paradise in which 'waters gushed', 'fruit trees grew' and 'flowers put forth a fairer hue', a world in which 'everything was strange and new'. More crucially for the boy who loses this world, there is the possibility that his 'lame foot would be speedily cured'. But he is too late. The music stops, he is alone 'outside the hill' and can only 'go now limping as before' in a grey world, bereft of playmates, 'And never hear of that country more'.[18]

An entrance into other worlds, however, is not an automatic guarantee for those who actually learn to read, for many children who learn to master the skills are not enraptured by their reading. Others, who come to reading as a joyous pursuit, can lose that joy when beset by the drudgery of the work ethic. This way literature does not hold the revelatory power which it should. It fails to gain the child entrance into other worlds. Even the great myths, legends, fairy tales, poems, novels, epics and plays can be reduced to a rubble of printed words to be scrambled over to complete the task. Thereby, revelations and entrances into other worlds are as distant as the stars. Yet they really are 'just at hand'.

Without the deep engagement of the imagination a person's life tends towards dullness or even anaesthesia and, if there is no deployment of imagination in reading, literature itself becomes a matter for decoding. Imagination needs to be active. Sensibility needs to be on the move. When they are, the extraordinary is found 'just at hand' or requires a mere 'moment' of travel. I am particularly struck by the idea of the 'other world' being present or right next to the here and now, and by the notion of its easy accessibility. With the right cultural assistance, almost every child can exchange the everyday for the 'other world', simply by turning the pages of a book. The wand wielded by turning the page will also lead to enhanced visionary powers within the child's imagination outside the pages of the book.

The active use of imagination

For a child the 'other worlds' of literature must sometimes be visited in active ways. Children are active by nature. Consequently, much of their reading needs to be active to affect their imaginations. In this sense, the reader's experience of literature involves activities of the conscious and unconscious similar to the writer's. I am arguing here for experiences of literature for children which gain them actual, imaginative entrance into the 'metaphoric worlds' of the writer who made them. I am arguing for a more dynamic, visionary engagement with fictions in schools. I am well aware that the current movement appears to be going in the opposite direction. It would be easy to characterise the possible dangers of this according to John Dewey's description of how ordinary experience can be

> ... infected with apathy, lassitude and stereotype. We get neither the impact of quality through sense nor the meaning of things through thought. The 'world' is too much with us as a burden or distraction. We are not sufficiently alive to feel the tang of sense nor yet to be moved by thought.[19]

According to Dewey, a vital aspect of imaginative experience, on the other hand, is a sense of a 'massing of values'. In literacy, the achievement of such 'massing of values' requires teachers and children to engage deeply and extensively with a work of literature. Literature then becomes not only a means through which to learn key skills but also a vehicle for developing understanding and wisdom about the human condition. It is the difference between cracking a code and engaging with a work of art. Dewey argues that through art '... meanings of objects that are otherwise dumb, inchoate, restricted and resisted are clarified and concentrated and not by thought working laboriously upon them, not by escape into a world of mere sense, but by creation of a new experience'.[20]

Applied to children and literature this 'new experience' is best achieved by that active behaviour, play. The value of works of quality in literature will be limited if we fail to mobilise this resource, so frequently abandoned once children have left the reception class. The play I am referring to here is that which engages fantasy elements and role-play, that which can broadly be described as 'enactment'. By 'fantasy' I mean 'visionary' as opposed to 'capricious', 'fantasy' as a 'mental image' which does not necessarily conform to all the details in the world outside, as we know it to be; 'fantasy' encompassing the ability to suspend our day-to-day view of how things are and speculate about how they might be. It is the elimination of 'fantasy' or 'fancy' which leads in Dickens's *Hard Times* to the emotional ruin of Gradgrind's daughter Louisa:

> 'Yet father, if I had been stone blind; if I had groped my way by my sense of touch and been free, while I knew other shapes and surfaces of things, to exercise my fancy somewhat, in regard of them, I should have been a million times wiser, happier, more loving, more contented, more innocent and human in all good respects than I am with the eyes I have.'[21]

The exercise of 'fantasy' or 'fancy' here is the exercise of the freedom to explore the essence of things up to and beyond their surface 'facts', the freedom to speculate, wonder, and make believe. This is seen as offering the possibility of greatly widened humanity. In this fiction Dickens presents a statement of 'the aesthetic', laying claim to it as a vital element to fullness of being, and the stakes are that high. Louisa, here, is unable to think for herself at a time of great personal crisis because the 'other world' of fantasy has been denied her.

It is possible that the greatest single danger coming from the National Literacy Strategy with its targets measured with the Standard Assessment Tasks is just this loss of autonomous feeling, thinking and expressing. It is possible that 'other worlds' may become 'out of bounds' in schools, as children are 'pressed' into the service of a government's aims and objectives. Certainly, literature in the National Literacy Strategy is hardly conceptualised as a doorway into other worlds. Notions about the sublime are unlikely to have had much space in the mind of John Stannard and his committee. Only teachers in their daily work can ameliorate such a danger.

Enactment projects

I am advocating here approaches to fiction in the primary school which encompass a wide range of activity. I have in mind far more than is implied by a series of literacy hours based on a fictional text. However, I am not proposing a rejection of the literacy strategy but rather proposing a model in which the word level, sentence level and text level activities are subsumed under more ambitious projects. These projects will involve extensive use of the arts and a sense of living with the experience, which resembles the kind enactment involved in the great ceremonies of world culture down the ages.

A good example of enactment through ceremony is provided by Black Elk, Holy Man of the Oglala Sioux who, at the age of nine, had his power vision. As an old, defeated man he told the story of it to the US poet John Neihardt. In this vision of the 'other world' Black Elk is spirited to a cloud world in a procession led by horses where he meets six deities known as 'the Grandfathers'. They give him power gifts: a wooden cup carrying the water of life; a healing herb; a peace pipe; and a bright red stick to 'stand in the centre of the nation's circle', where it will blossom. The Grandfathers evoke the life of the earth and of the spirit and reveal past and future. He learns prophetic songs and is shown key symbols.[22]

A myth is made through a special man's faculties and according to the patterns of his culture. Its significance is great for Black Elk but even greater for his culture. At sixteen Black Elk's power vision was turned into communal art, to become the possession of the tribe. The enactment of the vision by the tribe begins with two elders preparing a sacred teepee:

> . . . in the middle of the circle Bear Sings and Black Road set up a sacred teepee of bison hide and on it they painted pictures from my vision. On the west side they painted a bow and a cup of water; on the north, white geese and the herb; on the east, the daybreak star and the pipe; on the south, the flowering stick and the nation's hoop. Also they painted horses, elk and bison. Then over the door of the sacred teepee, they painted the flaming rainbow. It took them all day to do this and it was beautiful.[23]

Black Elk teaches the vision songs while his parents prepare the equipment. Horses are assembled as in the vision, riders chosen, and both painted to interpret the symbols. Six Grandfathers and four sacred virgins are chosen and a symbolic pattern is painted on the ground in the middle of the teepee. The dance begins with the singing of the songs, then Black Elk sees his vision again in the clouds. The riders re-enact the events of the dream, moving round the village. The tribe's involvement brings uplift for everybody. 'After the horse dance was over, it seemed that I was above the ground and did not touch it when I walked. I felt happy, for I could see that my people were all happier.'[24] So this communal enactment of the vision changes the way the people feel about themselves and this transmutation came not only from the vision but also from converting it into form.

The enactment of Black Elk's vision offers an uplifting model for the celebration of works of literature in schools in the sense that children may work both individually and together on a common project. Such communal endeavour, in which a vision – in this case from literature – is made into art and elevates the participants, provides the supreme model for the kind of engagement with literature in schools which children need. Malcolm Ross calls it the 'vernacular arts curriculum' which stresses 'the community or commonwealth of the arts and so would be constantly reinforcing their common roots in human need and human expression as well as their [the children's] social and political identity within the school.'[25]

The greatest moments in my own teaching have been generated when there has been a well-developed sense of solidarity between all members of the class, including myself. This in turn has led to a range of work clearly identifiable as a whole, a kind of vernacular art, when individual children's pieces of work cohere to make something which is collectively and recognisably in harmony.

Such projects can have a *renaissance* effect in a school. The discovery of great works of fiction, from other cultures as well as their own, can become a motor force for developing vernacular works. In the ways developed later in the book, works from oral cultures, classic works and modern children's fiction can be *vernacularised* or possessed and remade by children in their classrooms in a collective, expressive endeavour as in the following example from a contemporary British classroom.

A class of upper juniors is sharing the Old English narrative poem, *Beowulf*. The teacher acts as mediator between the children and the text, telling and reading the story and finding ways to intensify its power for them.[26] The morning after the first episode of the story she brings extracts of Stravinsky's *Rite of Spring*, which they listen to as if it is a film score for the story of Grendel's visit to Heorot and his grisly feast on King Hrothgar's men. The children are eager to hear this music over and over as it helps them to imagine the events in the story more intensely. Then comes the enactment, well prepared by the teacher in her plans. The scene is enacted in dance and the children's response is notable for its spontaneity yet its strong control, which creates an intensity in facial and bodily expression. The children convey a quality of feeling which is rivetting to the visitor and free of self-consciousness. Back in the classroom there is an animation which invigorates all other work that day.

This quality is invested in all forms of enactment which subsequently take place. The walls of the classroom grow rich with murals and large expressive paintings. The poems and stories written by the children are powerful responses which reveal an 'emotional quality of truth'. *Beowulf* was occupying and fulfilling the children's dreaming states. Parents ask the teacher about it when they call, eager to share in what is going on. The story and its various forms of enactment penetrate the expressive worlds of the children so that, when they travel in role to the great lake to kill Grendel's mother for wreaking terrible vengeance on Heorot for the death of her son, that moment is played with utter conviction and the story made to live more than a millennium after its composition. This teacher had so enthused her children with her transmission of this strange poem that they were able to release responses which, in the words of Maud Bodkin, quoting from Gilbert Murray, came from:

. . . a strange, unanalysed vibration below the surface, an under-current of desires and fears and passions, long slumbering yet eternally familiar, which have for thousands of years lain near the root of our most intimate emotions and been wrought into the fabric of our magical dreams.[27]

Secondary and tertiary worlds

If it were not for this potential for 'strange, unanalysed vibration', which all people have, a work such as *Beowulf* could not possibly inhabit the imaginations of contemporary children. Works like this are 'great' inasmuch as they are able to vibrate those 'desires and fears and passions' which lie 'below the surface'. On such occasions the reader makes contact with the humanity of the writer, storyteller or visionary and with the familiar world that we all share through this subconscious faculty. The writer, storyteller or visionary, by engaging with the world we all know, the primary world, makes something new out of the old and familiar. An 'other world' is created, a secondary world. According to Coleridge, the primary imagination is at work, and according to Auden, the works thus created are 'secondary worlds'. Auden sees in this the satisfaction of two complementary desires:

> Present in every human being are two desires, a desire to know the truth about the primary world, the given world outside ourselves in which we are born, live, love, hate and die, and the desire to make new secondary worlds of our own or, if we cannot make them ourselves, to share in the secondary worlds of those who can.[28]

The Oglala Sioux were sharing Black Elk's 'secondary world' and being invigorated by it, their individual creativity realised within his 'secondary world'. For this reason the importance of Black Elk's vision was its transforming effect upon the tribe. Black Elk's 'secondary world' was so stimulating because it bore immediately on the whole tribe's primary world, and their 'desire to know the truth' about it. This is true also of such works as *Beowulf* in relation to the contemporary child. The 'secondary world' of a work of art is not reality itself but a fragment of it removed, recast, transformed and framed, and such secondary worlds will be 'great' insofar as they assist our first desire of knowing the 'truth about the primary world'.

When children tell and write their own stories they make 'new secondary worlds of their own' which will tell truths about the primary world. When they enact, tell and write stories derived from the secondary worlds of others they not only 'share in [those] secondary worlds', but also create something else new. These can be called 'tertiary worlds', as in this story by ten-year-old Imogen working on a project based on Homer's *The Odyssey*:

> Look at this dirty sheet. I wouldn't be surprised if it had been under this couch for a god's century. Still I mustn't grumble. It will be a good day out . . . What's that I hear? My mistress asks her father, the great sea-king Alcinoos, for a mule to pull the cart she promised to use. Phew, as least I won't have to walk. When dawn spread out her fingertips of rose we stood outside the palace . . . The green blue glossy riverbed does its work well. The thick dust floats downstream . . . What is it? A wild man. At least he holds an olive branch to cover his nakedness. I bet he is ashamed, a middle-age man in his prime.[29]

Here, Imogen imagines she is one of Nausikaa's maids, present when Odysseus is discovered naked on the island. She makes the narrative material her own by creating a different language from Homer's, the language of homely conversation. However, she also maintains its language links with the original by using Homer's language devices, known as epithets, 'the great sea-king Alcinoos' and 'When dawn spread our her fingertips of rose'. She uses fragments of the original while creating a fiction which is distinctively her own, the fiction of the maid's thoughts in response to an event involving the greater characters. She creates a third reality, a tertiary world grafted onto the secondary world she is experiencing.

Reading the 'other worlds' of fiction in a primary classroom requires the kind of all-consuming involvement described here and in the rest of this book. This will naturally lead to the creation of new work, as well as the closer, more investigative scrutiny of texts recommended in the Strategy 'Framework'. The alternative, which has led to the reactions discussed at the opening of this chapter, is the superficial glossing of texts to fulfill lesser objectives than the life-enhancing power that literature can afford.

References and notes

1. Gantz, J. (1976) 'Pwyll Prince of Dyfed', *The Mabinogion*, 47. Harmondsworth: Penguin.
2. 'Labour hits back at 'elitist' attackers', (July 23, 1999) *Times Educational Supplement.*
3. Bateson, P. (August 31, 1999) 'Let children play', *The Guardian.*
4. Uttley, A. (1967) 'Little Red Fox and the Unicorn', *Little Red Fox Stories*, 43–77. London: Heinemann Books.
5. Winnicott, D. W. (1971) *Playing and Reality*, 12. London: Tavistock Publications.
6. Winnicott (1971) 47.
7. Winnicott (1971) 17.
8. Winnicott (1971) 16.
9. Winnicott (1971) 6.
10. Hill, E. *Spot's Friends.* London: William Heinemann.
11. Goodall, J. S. *Creepy Castle.* London: André Deutsch Publishers.
12. Bruna, D. (1962) *Animal Book.* London: Methuen Publications.
13. Pienkowski, J. *Shapes.* Harmondsworth: Puffin Books.
14. Stannard, J. (1998) *The National Literacy Strategy Framework for Teaching*, 5. London: Department for Education and Employment.
15. Stannard (1998) 2.
16. Smith, F. (1978) *Reading*, 1. Cambridge: Cambridge University Press.
17. Smith (1978) 9.
18. Browning, R. (1941) 'The Pied Piper of Hamelin', in *Poetry and Prose.* London: Oxford University Press.
19. Dewey, J. (1934) *Art as Experience*, 260. New York: Minton, Balch and Company Publishers.
20. Dewey (1934) 56.
21. Dickens, C. (1969) *Hard Times*, 240. Harmondsworth: Penguin Books.
22. Neihardt, J. G. (1974) *Black Elk Speaks*, 41. London: Abacus Paperbacks.
23. Neihardt (1974) 118.
24. Neihardt (1974) 126.
25. Ross, M. (1984) *The Aesthetic Impulse*, 44. London: Pergamon Press.
26. Alexander, M. (1973) *Beowulf.* Harmondsworth: Penguin Books.
27. Bodkin, M. (1934) *Archetypal Patterns in Poetry*, 2. London: Oxford University Press.
28. Auden, W. H. (1954) *Secondary Worlds*, 1. London: Faber and Faber.
29. Carter, D. B. (1987) *The Odyssey Project.* Mold: Clwyd County Council.

Chapter Two

Storytelling and literacy

KIRA: What are those funny marks?
JEN: This is all writing.
KIRA: What is writing?
EN: Words that stay. My master told me.[1]

Words look after themselves

In the history of human communication literacy is a new development. According to recent archaeological findings in Egypt, 'records of linen and oil deliveries on clay tablets' have been carbon dated to about 5300 years ago.[2] Although this may seem a very long time ago, it represents about three per cent of the history of human discourse. The other 97 per cent has been conducted through the medium of talk alone and one of the most highly developed products of all the millennia of talking is storytelling. This art, only revived in the western world during the last 15 years or so, reached heights of elaboration which were only fully discovered in the 1930s through the researches of Milman Parry in the Balkans.[3]

Parry's work led him to conclude that the storytelling of Homer was entirely conducted orally, that *The Iliad* and *The Odyssey*, which literary critics down the ages have discussed as great works of literature, were not strictly 'literature' at all. Neither work, claimed Parry, was composed through writing. They were composed through talking, or, more accurately, through singing. They were improvisations, like jamming in jazz, and one performance was never the same as another. That such vast and magnificent works of art such as these should be composed in this way is almost beyond the comprehension of the literate mind, which tends to dismiss non-literacy as an inferior state. Yet the consensus view among Greek scholars since Milman Parry's pioneering work is that Homer, whoever he was or they were, composed them entirely without any form of reading or writing.[4]

Now this is hard to imagine. Nothing even jotted down as an *aide-mémoire*. No notes. No cribs. In order to approach an understanding I will recall a workshop with Hugh Lupton of 'The Company of Storytellers'. Hugh was attempting to provide us with ways of memorising stories so that we could retell them to others. 'Try to see the pictures', he urged, 'then the words will look after themselves.' This was pictures-into-words, which would, if the story was well told, put words-into-pictures in the imaginations of an audience. He also talked about the surface structure of an orally told folk or fairy tale and how certain fixed verbal arrangements such as 'Fee, Fi, Fo, Fum, I smell the blood of an Englishman' appear. Hugh said that such phrases float to the surface during the storyteller's performance, providing another kind of fixed point in addition to the mental pictures.[5]

So the mental pictures and orally remembered rhymes or rhythmic phrases were providing Hugh and, hopefully, us with cribs or prompts which would not require the act of writing. When Hugh performed his stories for us it was also noticeable just how important gesture and facial expression were as aids to his memory. All this may seem a far cry from Homer singing to an audience of early Greeks but it provides pointers to that more complex verbal artistry. What I am attempting to imply is that the tendency and ability to tell stories is within us all and is a valuable verbal and mental asset much neglected since the dominance of the printing press.

Hugh Lupton's process is relatively straightforward and not entirely oral. Being actually literate, Hugh has built his story repertoire by reading stories as well as listening to them. However, there still exist in Britain storytellers who are preliterate, and Hugh has learnt stories from them.[6] Preliterate verbal artists are more widespread in other parts of the world. The work of Ruth Finnegan in West Africa and the South Pacific provides extensive evidence of this. Her study of the Limba people and various inhabitants of the South Pacific region shows how accomplished this verbal art can be.[7]

It was Milman Parry's study of Yugoslavian oral poets in the 1930s which convinced him that Homer was not a writer. When a literary critic and poet like Ezra Pound wrote in praise of Homer he had in mind the greatest man of letters, a Shakespeare, only even greater. The astonishing thing is that letters probably had no meaning at all for Homer. His medium was not the visual code of letters making words and words making phrases. It was of units of spoken language and these were not even 'made up' by Homer himself. The making of a work of verbal art through the medium of oral language is much more of a shared act.

Homer's formulae

Extensive researches into contemporary Yugoslavian oral poetry led Milman Parry to believe that Homer's use of the traditional epithet was convincing evidence of his being an oral poet. The epithet is similar in function to Hugh Lupton's 'Fee, Fi, Fo, Fum' example, although it is an adjectival phrase rather than the speech words of a character or a song. It is usually descriptive of the characters. Every time a certain character appears, speaks or acts, the introduction of his or her name is accompanied by one or other of the epithets associated with that character's origins or persona, as in these examples from *The Odyssey*:

> The *grey-eyed goddess* Athena . . .
> Zeus, *the father of the gods and men* . . .
> When Dawn spread out her fingertips of rose . . .
> Now Zeus, *the lord of cloud* . . .
> Odysseus, *the kingly man*, replied . . .
> At once Odysseus, *the great tactician* . . .[8]

The epithet, as I say, was the key to Parry's hypothesis, but in terms of Homer's compositional process it was one component of what was a formulaic method. The various formulae, tuned to fit the hexameter, were like chapter headings. Like some mighty novel or narrative verse, like Tolstoy's *War and Peace* or Chaucer's *Canterbury Tales*, this thing of air would be constructed; and a vital part of the act of construction would be the audience. Homer's audience would know the epithets and the other formulae, would be well used to the various ways of the storyteller:

> From their earliest childhood, his audience must have heard again and again long recitations of epic poetry, poetry composed always in the same style. The diction of this poetry, accessible to the modern reader only by way of long study, was familiar to them in its smallest details.[9]

Homer's audience would be a most exacting one. Each member of it would have a discriminating ear, but what they would be listening for would not be the revelation of the poet's original thinking, nor even any 'particularised meaning'. Parry insists that we should avoid ascribing the kind of 'profundity and the finesse' which we might 'admire in contemporary art'. This always ends, he claims, with us 'denigrating the habitual in order to praise the exceptional'.[10]

So, that is how Homer created his fictions before there was writing. It emerged out of a particular set of relationships between poet and audience far removed from our own. It is the finest example of that art, the noble end of what was the only vehicle for creating and communicating fictions as well as true stories. Often, of course, it would be difficult to tell the difference between the two. Great travelling verbal artists such as Homer were practising their skills throughout the world before alphabets eroded their art and, ultimately, replaced it with fictions in letters or literature. So, too, were ordinary folk by their own firesides, in the street or public house. The former is now known as mythology, the latter as fairy tales, folk tales or legends.

The listener inside you

Throughout this book I will be asserting the value of oral storytelling both to the development of children's oracy and literacy skills. However, before this we need to consider the particular qualities of oral storytelling. To assist me in this I turn to the work of director Peter Brook. When directing a play based on *The Mahabharata*, the Indian epic, his basic idea was that it should appear as a story being told and that the enactments would be introduced each time by an actor in role as the storyteller. This concept led Brook into thinking about the nature of the storyteller in relation to the stories he tells. In an interview he gave at the time, he talked of *internal* as well as *external* approaches to storytelling. In other words, he urged his actors to perform and to listen at one and the same time. This, he believed, would make the story alive, would make the retelling of it a rediscovery:

> I think that the whole question of quality in speech, quality in tone of voice, depends on whether or not a certain two-way listening is there. As you tell a story, can you listen to it so that there are two listeners? There's the listener in front of you who is hearing it maybe for the first time, and there's also the listener inside you, who's not enjoying hearing the story for the

hundredth time, lazily, like somebody who likes the sound of his voice, but who has the listening of someone re-appreciating and reopening himself to the story. Then there is two-way listening. You are listening to what you're telling to the other person and you are genuinely rediscovering it.[11]

Now this would probably have been much easier for oral poets like Homer to do than for Brook's actors. Although he only chooses the finest actors they are products of a literate society and unlikely to have the massive range of oral skills or prodigious memories of the preliterate poets.

The oral poet, according to Albert Lord, would need at least a day to digest new material before being able to repeat it. This new story would 'sink into his own store of themes and formulas' and would not re-emerge verbatim.[12] It would be changed, fitted into the poet's own flow, maybe with one or two stolen epithets, but even these enlarged or truncated to suit his metre: and all the time, surely, he would be listening and performing. In addition, the involvement of audience would be crucial. It is audience that marks the most important difference between oral poet and writer. As Ong observes 'The writer's audience is always a fiction. The writer must set up a role in which absent and often unknown readers can cast themselves'.[13] Part of the story's nature for the oral poet would be its adaptation to the conditions pertaining during performance, the audience's reaction and, in Homer's time, their active participation. Storytelling would, therefore, be 'composition-in-performance' and the poet would not be thought of as author or creator, but as a mediator between the audience and the Muse.

Responding to the spoken word

My harking back across the millennia to another time and society may appear to have little relevance to children in the twenty-first century learning within the strictures of The National Literacy Strategy. Yet, curiously, the very developments in technology that have advanced writing and, particularly, printing, have advanced the cause of orality. Most young children spend more time responding to the spoken word than the written and, too often, the two forms are seen to be in conflict. So, the lament that children are not making enough progress in their reading because of watching too much television has become one of the signature tunes of the educational project. This need not be so. The child listening to the story can become the child telling the story. Television can be seen as a source of stories, one way of receiving pleasure and instruction through the word. Society can provide several other examples and school more than most.

The need to share stories is central to us all. Indeed, we do it willy-nilly. In our literate society, however, such storytelling will relate chiefly to written forms. Jackanory storytellers, for instance, learn their lines even though they seem to be telling their stories spontaneously. Such memorisation has its place, but far more valuable will be storytelling which is improvised, which is closer to the acts of the oral poets. Introduced early enough and made part of a child's general education, the telling of tales would resemble such acts still to be found in other parts of the world. In the Bougainville Straits, for instance, a storytelling process exists, which provides a significant example for our children:

Here the stories are not unchangeable wholes, handed down in fixed form through oral tradition, but rather a series or combination of 'motives' – themes and plots. One storyteller will put these together in one way, another in a different way, so that there is not one final and 'correct' version of any tale – only the way the story is put together by an individual narrator on a particular occasion.[14]

Such a framework enables children to make a story more readily, unlike the request sometimes heard in schools simply to 'write a story'. This latter pedagogy presupposes that the child already contains the suitable themes and plots inside his head. When various narrow versions of Star Wars are the result, who can complain?

Yet themes and plots which matter to a school of children are often available in many forms. There are the handed-down tales, the personal anecdotes and reminiscences of members of the older generation and various aspects of local history. These can be made by an imaginative teacher into a stockpot for storytelling. Objects and places within a school's hinterland are sometimes resonant with themes, whether these be in buildings or in natural phenomena. Many ideas, themes and plots are also generated during the natural course of school life with its lessons, its assemblies and its general meeting of people from different backgrounds.

'The Storytelling Stone'

As part of their professional life teachers may also actively seek stories from the vast collection which has been rescued from the dying oral traditions of the world. The wise teacher will seek to create such cross-currents of story within the classroom and always be on the look-out for new opportunities. One such was provided by a Theatre in Education company. This was a deliberate attempt by the company to promote storytelling. The story of this initiative is best told starting near its end.

A troubled eight-year-old boy is standing in the hall of his school, holding a large pebble. In front of the whole class, this boy, who earlier refused to take part, saying that he had no story to tell, starts to tell his tale. He has not touched pencil or paper the whole day. But he has watched actors telling stories in role and this has emboldened him. He begins and soon is holding us all on the thread of his narrative, holding the 'storytelling stone' close to him. In this way he tells the story of a hero in possession of a huge key, who locks in a cellar the members of his family. This is to punish them for going off with other partners. He leaves for Australia, taking the key with him, and discovers a chest filled with treasure. Before he can take it he must defend it against a man called 'Dragon'. Having accomplished this feat, the treasure is his. He has arrived at a form of empowerment, if only for this fleeting moment.

The stock of themes and plots out of which this story was made, was supplied by the two actors who had earlier appeared as storytelling vagrants in a sandy hollow of sparse bushes and stones. Their language, too, was sparse. Their play, like a piece of Beckett or Pinter, told much without words, particularly when the two encountered a third character who lived in a bivouac of sticks and sacks. All three characters were difficult to pin down, but none more so than this troubled character who suddenly emerged from his hovel. When he staggered out, obviously distressed, he won the children's sympathy immediately. He had lost his memory and the children were invited to help to find out about his unhappy life story. There were clues: blood on his arm, a ring, the picture of a young woman, and a large, dragon-headed key. After much questioning by the other two characters, using questions supplied by the children, the sad stranger wrote 'Forget' in the sand with a stick.

The play ended with none of its problems solved. Solutions were to be found in the children's orally-composed stories. To assist this the actors created a powerful atmosphere in the composition session later in the day. One played a haunting melody on a recorder while the children closed their eyes and began creating pictures in their minds. So many ambiguities about the characters abounded and the material was so well crafted that the opportunities were endless. The three main objects – ring, picture and key – have archetypal significance and stories redolent of *Romeo and Juliet*, *Hamlet* and *Romulus and Remus* emerged. In among the long journeys, shipwrecks, loss of hearth and home, and exile, were issues of contemporary significance: divorce, the breakup of families, children being abandoned. Each story, however, was different. Here is the start of one of them:

> There was once a bad king and queen who made their son a servant. And so he wanted to get revenge so he took his mother's ring while she was not looking. And there was only one key to the castle and that was unguarded so he took that too. He did all these things to make his mother upset like she had made him upset. Then came his sister Princess Angelica. She was his favourite sister so he told her that he would go to the desert and there he would stay . . .[15]

This was composed orally and performed before the whole class and the theatre company. It was the first occasion for this child to perform in such a way, entirely without recourse to writing. It reveals, I believe, the potential of a verbal art form which is thousands of years older than writing. If acknowledged as having value and put into practice as part of children's literacy education, the benefits would reverberate across the whole range of children's development as articulate, literate and autonomous human beings. Regular opportunities to engage in storytelling would have effects upon verbal and nonverbal memory, narrative structuring, character depiction through the use of epithet and descriptions of characters' actions, lyrical stillness, narrative pacing and narrative momentum. Such a range of skills and awareness are essential features in the literate person's understanding and enjoyment of prose fiction, balladic verse and non-fictional story. It strikes me that such habits would greatly accelerate the reading development of regular participants in them, let alone the fluency of their speech.

Storytellers don't forget their lines

> But writing, with all its mystery, came to the singer's people and eventually someone approached the singer and asked him to tell the song so that he could write down the words . . . it was the strangest performance he had ever given.[16]

A travelling theatre company was having its 'evening of storytelling' videoed for use in schools. All was going well, despite the lack of a live audience. These were actors, who thrived on the establishment of a vibrant rapport with an intimate audience, but here they were acting to camera with a handful of people among cables, cases, boxes and a battery of lights. One or two began to fluff or even forget lines as fatigue set in. The actor-director of the company suddenly said 'I've forgotten my lines' and could not believe it. This was the first time he had forgotten them and the production was in the final week of rehearsal. A younger actor, who was taking the lead in one of the stories, mispronounced a word and halted for a rerun. The particular word had to be spoken correctly, and the actor-director had, for a moment, lost his particular words. The distractions of the unfamiliar situation had caused these problems, which lasted a few minutes.

To the company this was a tiresome irritation in an otherwise successful theatre piece. To me, a spectator, the situation was full of interesting parallels, contrasts and questions. The source material for the plays/storytellings, although mainly from folk and fairy tales in the oral tradition, were brought to the actors in a book. This book became the basis for a script, even though this script was arrived at through various acts of devising and improvising. Because the words were fixed, more or less, they had to be remembered. They were the main, although not the only, element in the act of telling. Even the parts of the plays which involved one actor telling a story, sitting on a chair, had to be performed from a memorised text because of the context of cues for lighting changes and for the responses from the other actors, some of which were essential to the meanings which the company wanted to draw from the stories.[17]

Even if the working process had been based solely on improvisation, the plays would still have reached a fixed and final text because of the theatrical demands which were incumbent upon a company of actors. This clearly is a different tradition from that of the oral storyteller. They are two different forms of discourse. Even those scenes in Peter Brook's *Mahabharata* in which a character tells tales are not storytelling in the way this was done by performers of old. Brook's actors were in role as storytellers within a play. Even they could have forgotten their lines, whereas it is unthinkable for an oral storyteller to forget his because the lines don't exist until he projects them into the air.

The actors in the travelling company were experiencing difficulties due to the pressures brought by the change of medium. Cameras require different performances from a live audience. No doubt, in the early stages of the creation of literatures, the singer also experienced some kind of initial destabilisation when he turned up at the writer's desk. Everything that assisted the singer would have been missing:

> There was no music and no song, nothing to keep him to the regular beat except the echo of previous singings and the habit they had formed in his mind. Without these accompaniments it was not easy to put the words together as he usually did.[18]

Worse still, there would be no flow, no onward move from one idea into the next, for 'now he had to stop very often for the scribe to write down what he was saying, after every line or even after part of a line. This was difficult, because his mind was far ahead.'[19]

The great difference, of course, between the actors and the singer is that for the actors the video session was a minor, temporary difficulty, whereas for the singer it was the beginning of the end of one tradition in verbal art and the birth of another. And the two are distinctly different, even more different than theatre and film. The whole method of composition is different, the mental states of the artists are different, their relationships with the surrounding culture different. The key to these differences lies in the massive changes brought by the invention of letters, of writing and the printing press.

Singing, telling and writing

The singers and the tellers of folk stories were guardians of their cultures. Their contribution was to maintain it in roughly its original forms. They transmitted the values, hopes, fears and philosophies of the people within their stories and a performance would be judged by its power to touch the moment with magic, to weave a spell over the audience and make the members of it feel glad to be part of their culture and together in it. A great epic performance would bind the people together, strengthening the culture and through it the resolution of the people to withstand any forces that might be pitched against it. The context of performance was, therefore, even more important than the words themselves. Even *The Odyssey* was not composed as a piece of literature but was newly composed over and over for each audience and for the purpose of uniting them. Meaning was related to context and language served the communication of the meanings the people needed and wanted to hear.

On the other hand, composition through writing, in the words of Ong, 'concentrates meaning in language itself'[20], creating infinite possibilities for the peculiarities of the individual verbal artist to be expressed. The act of composition is a lone act; it brings into play the verbal artist's inner world to a much more significant level. The artist's words, also, stand apart from their audience and can remain so for ever and still have existence, even though they are dead for audiences. Furthermore, although apparently dead, they can be brought to life like seeds buried deep in the ground: '. . . the deadness of the text, its removal from the living human lifeworld, its rigid visual fixity, assures its endurance and its potential for being resurrected into limitless living contexts by a potentially infinite number of living readers.'[21] The words have a life of their own, whereas the words of an oral poet live and die in the moment.

The development of literature, therefore, meant that verbal art was no longer restricted to individual moments of performance, which were social moments. The writer could explore other worlds, particularly the worlds within his own imagination, as Havelock claims:

> By separating the knower from the known, writing makes possible increasingly articulate introspectivity, opening the psyche as never before not only to the external objective world quite distinct from itself but also to the interior self against whom the objective world is set.[22]

The writer's process is, therefore, a private pursuit, his audience largely imagined, the oral poet's entirely public, his audience always there before him at the moment of composition.

So, writing 'came to the singer's people' and a new way of composing was invented. No longer was the moment of composition the moment of performance. A gap developed and even the sense of performance itself was reduced. The verbal artist now would work alone on his compositions, fixing them forever. Previously, the variation in his work would have occurred from one performance to the next. Variation now would depend on the response of the reader. Being fixed in the words, which have a life of their own, the verbal artist's works are open to interpretation, to individual response.

This is the case no matter how hard the writer tries to avoid it. So the work, having left the pen of the writer and entered the public domain ceases to belong to the writer to all intents and purposes, as Easthope observes: 'It is embodied in language, the peculiar possession of the public, and it is about the human being, an object of public knowledge.'[23] Being fixed, a text has what Jacques Derrida calls 'materiality' and, therefore, 'can never be fully permeated by conscious intention – the text will always mean for its readers something other than it means for its author'.[24]

Children engaging with the two traditions

The implications of this for the development of children's skills as readers and writers are extensive. Children's response to a work in which language itself is, as it were, in the background (storytelling) will be significantly different from their response to one in which language is more in the foreground. They are, however, of equal importance. Children need to engage with both kinds of verbal form to develop fully as users of their language. When a child engages with an oral story, or with any literary experience in which the text itself is in the background and the story in the foreground, he will need to create with words he already has when retelling, enacting or writing. So, for instance, if that child has only the bare bones of, say, a legend, the opportunity exists for him to fill it out with his own words, irrespective of the words in which he received it. These words in the air are transparent vessels, in which the story is carried to the listener's ear, rather than fixed elements demanding attention in their own right. Thus, opportunities are afforded to create a new species of fixed objects in language, to make written versions of the story, opportunities which writers such as Boccaccio, Shakespeare and Ted Hughes made use of. By offering them to children we are enabling them to participate in an act which is fundamental to a literate society.

The process of response will be somewhat different when a child engages with a literary text, a text in which language itself is in the foreground. The language in these cases cannot be ignored. Indeed to ignore such textually fixed language would be to treat the medium as transparent. To engage with a text means to take note of that text in terms both of its meaning and its materiality. There will, therefore, be appropriate and inappropriate ways of responding to it. To disregard this in schools is to lose a great deal of the educational potential which a work possesses for children. For instance, were a teacher to tell her children the story of *Macbeth*, shorn of Shakespeare's text and structure, it would be perfectly acceptable for the children to make of it what they would. However, this venture would have little, if anything, to do with Shakespeare. The highly wrought artistry in language, structure, stagecraft and characterisation which is inherent in Shakespeare's text makes certain demands. These demands cannot be met by questions such as 'How many children had Lady Macbeth?' Textual fixing makes the story more particular. There are, indeed, many stories similar to the basic story in *Macbeth*, but no other work of literary art resembles it. Therefore, when a child makes something out of this text, say, in writing, the child's writing is likely to mix elements from Shakespeare's text with elements of that child's response. This will make the educational experience for the child one which complements his writings from the oral tradition. A useful guiding principle, perhaps, would be that the

~~26~~

...e of art exercised in the creation of a text, the greater the responsibility ...d child to respond to the text in its fullness, rather than to one of its

...n writing stories

...ecome successful writers of fiction, children need an active imagination with which to invent other worlds. This will develop according to the amount of exposure they get to a broad range of genres and the ways teachers engage them with those stories. Their success will also be affected by their experiences of fiction outside of school, much of which will come from film, television and computer games. However, imagination will be developed more fully by the kinds of project described in Chapter 1 and developed in Chapters 4, 5 and 6, in which they are encouraged to live within other worlds.

There are also two more specific sets of abilities which need to be developed, if children are to make stories which will be read and enjoyed by other readers. They are a mastery of story structure and the development of personal style. These will also mature through exposure to various genres of fiction. However, this process will be accelerated if they receive a balanced exposure both to orally told stories and to literature. By exposure I mean that children listen to stories being told to them and read to them; that they regularly tell and write stories; and that they respond to these fictions through drama and the other arts.

Children's sense of story structure is, as it were, trained by listening to stories being told to them and by telling stories themselves, whereas the development of their personal style as writers of stories is affected by listening to stories being read to them and writing their own stories. In an interesting piece of research for a Master of Education dissertation, Catherine Carter claims:

> Research indicates that whereas listening to an oral storyteller introduces children to a flow of language and to a sense of structure, listening to texts being read aloud enriches children's vocabulary and increases their ability to compose complex written narratives of their own.[25]

Her research involved a class of children in a series of listening and writing activities in which stories were told and read equally. Carter shows that, even in a short space of time, the majority of children will reveal significant improvements in the structure and style of their story writing as a result of being exposed to the two distinctively different listening experiences. She concludes her research by asserting:

> The children studied in this research developed their skills as story writers through listening to stories being told to them, followed by listening to stories in the same genre being read aloud to them from good quality texts. Listening to stories being told to them provided them with a story structure. Listening to stories being read to them increased their control over the pace of the story and encouraged them to develop the evaluative aspects as well as their use of more complex sentences and literary language. Learning was more effective if storytelling activities preceded the use of a text.[26]

If in such a short space of time – a half term – and only through listening and writing activities, children can make visible progress as story writers, the implications of a more ambitious programme are profound indeed. The main claim of this book will be that by involving children in the kinds of project described in Chapter 1 and by engaging them extensively as receivers and makers of oral and written fictions, their development as writers of stories will be significantly advanced, particularly if this becomes part of a whole-school philosophy and approach. Furthermore, I will be claiming that the development of children's powers of logical deduction, creative imagination and their fluency as talkers, readers and writers will all benefit from such work.

References and notes

1. Henson, J. and Ox, F. (1982), *The Dark Crystal*, UK. [film].
2. "Tax form' tablets revise history of writing' (December 16, 1998) London: *The Guardian.*
3. Parry M. (1971) *The Making of Homeric Verse.* London: Oxford University Press.
4. Parry (1971).
5. Hugh Lupton's workshop was for teachers wishing to develop oral storytelling in their classrooms. Hugh introduced a number of techniques for remembering and retelling stories.
6. Hugh named Duncan Williamson, the Scottish storyteller.
7. Finnegan, R. (1988) *Literacy and Orality*, 45–122. London: Basil Blackwell Publishers.
8. Fitzgerald, R. (trans.) (1961), *The Odyssey.* London: Collins Harvill.
9. Parry (1971) 129.
10. Parry (1971) 141.
11. Brook, P. (1989) *The 1989 International Storytelling Festival Souvenir Programme*, 9–10. London: The South Bank Centre.
12. Lord, A. B. (1960) *The Singer of Tales*, 32. New York: Harvard University Press.
13. Ong, W. J. (1982) *Orality and Literacy*, 102. London: Routledge.
14. Finnegan (1988) 92.
15. This story was told during a workshop conducted by members of Outreach Theatre Company as part of their show, 'The Storytelling Stone', which toured Clwyd during the Spring Term,1990. The Company was made up of Kevin Lewis (director), Tracy Cavalier, Stuart Seller and David Lloyd-Skillern.
16. Lord (1960) 124.
17. This was an attempt to make a film record of Outreach Theatre Company's Christmas storytelling show, 'As the Sun Sets', in December 1989. The Company consisted of Kevin Lewis (director), Tracy Cavalier, Rhys Ifans, David Lloyd-Skillern, Alison Wynne and Stuart Seller.
18. Lord (1960) 124.
19. Lord (1960) 124.
20. Ong (1982) 106.
21. Ong (1982) 77.
22. Havelock, E. (1986) *The Muse Learns to Write*, 64. New Haven: Yale University Press.
23. Easthope, A. (1983) *Poetry as Discourse*, 5. London: Methuen Publications.
24. Havelock (1986) 58.
25. Carter (1998) *Story Writing Abilities*, 15. Wales: Unpublished MEd Dissertation.
26. Carter (1998) 64.

Chapter Three

Ways of working with fiction

Teacher as intermediary

In the current climate of strategies and target-setting it is easy to forget that an essential characteristic of a teacher's role is the development of a human relationship with children. At the beginning of the new millennium it is also remarkable how closely the contemporary pedagogical relationship resembles that which existed between the elders of preliterate societies and their children. As with our distant ancestors, teachers are there to help interpret the mysteries of the world for young minds and equip them with skills necessary to assume a purposeful role in the society.

The elders of the ancient tribes would make consistent use of story as part of their 'teaching'. As discussed earlier, a story contained the collected wisdom of the tribe just as the printed word – along with the photograph, the sound and film recording – carries the collected wisdom of post-modern society. The storytelling elders, therefore, were intermediaries between the children and the tribe's collected wisdom, and the same can be said of teachers. Teachers are intermediaries and the best teachers are not so much those who hit targets, but rather those who tell the most memorable stories.

Teachers like these can make the stories of 'materials and their properties' into adventures just as easily as they can take their children with Odysseus during his 20 year journey. In their mouths and hands the story of multiplication can be exciting during the same morning as they take their children into the world of 'Jack and the Beanstalk'. Teachers such as these will also hit the targets set for them, but will achieve far more.

The power of story

Story is the most powerful means for teaching anything. No wonder then that most commercials construct stories to promote their products. Think of the fairy tale world built around the launch of the latest car, which takes the new owner to undreamed of fulfilments. Banal these narratives might be, but they work!

The poet and story-writer Ted Hughes recognised the potency of story in his much printed essay, 'Myth and Education'. Here he writes that a child '. . . takes possession of a story as what might be called a unit of imagination . . . In attending to the world of story there is the beginning of imaginative and mental control. There is the beginning of a form of contemplation.'[1]

Hughes also claims that, once a story is learnt and becomes part of our mental resources, certain key words can evoke the whole story. These key words may be the title of the story or the name of a hero, the name of a place or an object. They are keys to unlock other existences, other worlds. The words themselves assume greater power to evoke not only the story but many of the associations which accompany the experience of it. It is, perhaps, in these associations that the power of story is most potent. It is also here that the teacher as intermediary can fulfil her role most lastingly.

When we unlock and enter the other world of a story we may make that world particular to ourselves through the range of associations with aspects of our lives that the story can evoke. So, that other world may become for us, at one and the same time, shared and personal. But it requires a form of vigorous imagination in children for this to be achieved.

Associations and personal response

The German philosopher Hans-Georg Gadamer in his essay 'On the contribution of poetry to the search for truth' illustrates the way personal response through association can work by looking at a certain staircase that the character, Smerdjakov, falls down in Dostoevsky's novel *The Brothers Karamazov.*

> The staircase that Smerdjakov falls down plays a major role in the story. Everyone who has read the book will remember this scene and will 'know' what the staircase looks like. Not one of us has exactly the same image of it and yet we all believe that we see it quite vividly. It would be absurd to ask what the staircase 'intended' by Dostoevsy really looked like. Through the way which the writer succeeds in rousing the imagination of every reader to construct an image so that he thinks he sees exactly how the stairs turn to the right, descend for a couple of steps, and then disappear into the darkness below. If someone else says that it turns left, descends for six steps, and then is lost in the darkness, he is obviously just as much in the right. By not describing the scene in any more detail than he has, Dostoevsky stimulates us to construct an image of the stairs in our imagination.[2]

Now this illustrates not only the subtleties of Dostoevsky's art of literary storytelling but also that when readers fully engage with a fiction their imaginations actively make associations. When such associations are made a sort of trace is left in the mind of the reader, which often remains as a permanent part of the pattern of imagination.

Such associations might work as follows. The writer describes, say, a certain stand of trees, which perhaps evokes a significant atmosphere or is situated where an important incident takes place in the fiction. For his or her part, the reader does not see exactly what the writer sees. That description provides a framework or a set of directions for the imagination to work on. The writer's stand of trees will be replaced slightly either by an actual stand of trees experienced by the reader and stored up, or by a kind of synthesis of stands of trees seen and imagined. So, the writer's stand of trees attracts and unites what might be disparate perceptions into a wholly new perception, which is imbued by the fiction with a new set of feelings and pictures.

This can be a powerful, life-enhancing experience and the new perception is somewhat different for each reader. Unless they have all seen David Lean's film, no one reader's mental picture of the graveyard where Pip encounters Magwich in *Great*

Expectations will be the same. Yet all readers whose imaginations are sufficiently vigorous will be powerfully affected by Dickens's description, characterisation and development of the plot around it. The perceptions of all readers will have much in common, so that they will be able to respond together, showing a similar mixture of fascination and terror as Pip makes his way across the marshes with the file and the 'vittles'.

Developing the vigorous imagination

A vigorous imagination cannot be taken for granted. Although it is a gross error whenever a teacher says a certain child has 'no imagination', it is true to say that many children do not necessarily engage their imaginations with the stories they meet in texts. Possibly this is because their access to story is more often through a medium which is easier to engage with – film and television. A more likely explanation, however, is that such children have not received the right kinds of assistance to activate their imaginations.

Children in their primary schools need more than seven years of literacy hours, however well planned and recorded such sessions are. They need more than storytime at the end of the day, however pleasurable this might be. Children are not naturally sedentary creatures, even though many do find it nice to curl up with a book. To become reflective beings they need actions to reflect upon. In order to enter the other worlds of fiction and to develop as lifelong readers children need action. This chapter will describe the types of action required, much of which has been part of the school curriculum for years. But first, an example.

'The Rime of the Ancient Mariner'

A class of Year 5 and Year 6 children is experiencing Coleridge's narrative poem, 'The Rime of the Ancient Mariner'.[3] The pattern of activity is simple. The class teacher reads the poem in episodes to the children, explaining and questioning as she does so. The children recite some of the verses, discuss what they mean and explain their ideas to each other. They write regularly, often in free verse forms. Sometimes the topics they write about are merely brief quotations from the text such as 'Water, water everywhere' or 'ice was all around'. Such starting points enable the children to reconstruct the drama and the vivid visual descriptions in their own words and there is great variation, as follows:

1. Water, water everywhere.
Neck brittle and still,
no chin wagging
or joyful laughing.
Instead a dismal
sheen of silence.
As dry as a stone
a ghost ship is becalmed. (David)

2. Water, water everywhere
my mouth is dry as crisp.
Water, water everywhere

the wood is hot as coal.
Water, water everywhere
blood is hot as desert sand. (Lee – extract)

The two pieces, written in response to the same classroom experience, show significant differences. David's is more evaluative. The scene is 'dismal' with all human intercourse gone. There is no conversation ('chin wagging') and no 'joyful laughter'. Lee's surveys the scene, providing examples to add to those of Coleridge in a series of similes about the effects of the heat.

The children also paint these scenes regularly, often in semi-abstract forms which embody key images: a mast among ice with a white star or bird in a black sky. More telling, perhaps, is the regular work in dance and drama. This work ranges from improvisations of the mariner 'stopping' people to tell his story to more abstract representations of the movement – or lack of it – of the ship and the visions. After a dance session exploring the vision of 'spectre bark', Ben writes,

It glitters and shines in the sun's rays.
But what's this? Death in a cloak.
As black as burnt ash and Life and Death
playing games with our souls.
And thrusting her sails
like a raging torrent did below
but no wind did whistle.
The ship so fine like the lightest
note it glides the surface.
Our hopes did fall to a
bottomless pit and our faces
did crack with horror and fear.
And she came closer with a vile smile.

In this piece Ben has re-presented the scene from Coleridge in his own way as a result of the actions he has taken in dance and drama, but has not described the actions themselves. When he writes of the falling of hope and the cracking of faces he describes the feelings that accompany the actions or, more precisely, the feelings accompanying his recollection of those actions. Thus, there are three levels to his response:

- to the teacher's presentation
- to the enactments in dance and drama
- to his reflection on both.

These examples of children's writing demonstrate imaginations on the move as a result of the actions which the teacher has set in motion. They also show the variation of response from one imagination to the next as individual 'readers' reconstruct the other world of Coleridge's narrative poem.

The teacher's preparation

Mention planning to any primary teacher and eyebrows immediately rise. The last ten years or so have seen the biggest growth in school bureaucracy since universal education began. Stories of boxloads of documents passed from head teachers to registered inspectors prior to the OFSTED inspection and of planning sessions into the early hours are common. Every new educational initiative comes with its plan, usually in a glossy format, well bound and crisp. The teacher's file or record book, which used to be a kind of enthusiast's diary, is now more likely to consist of grids and learning objectives.

For these reasons I use the word 'preparation' instead of planning. What I have in mind is something a little different. I am thinking of a teacher who is mentally and creatively prepared for immersing her children in an experience which could change their lives for the better. I am thinking about standards here, but not merely standards as measured by tests. I am also thinking of standards of involvement, in which children's commitment, excitement and creative endeavour are mobilised.

The well-prepared teacher will enjoy the work of fiction she intends to introduce into her classroom. She will reject that which does not excite her and will have ambitions which may seem too high for her children. Such high ambition both honours the children and raises opportunities for their intellectual and emotional development. The well-prepared teacher will also have anticipated the opportunities that a work of fiction has for a whole range of learning across literacy and the arts. When she writes her plans – as she must – these possibilities will be integral to them. Most of all, however, she will have practised presenting the text to the children sufficiently so that their experience of it is memorable. She will attempt to represent the characters in the way she speaks their words. This does not require a master of regional dialects so much as someone who can bring gentleness, aggression or fear into her voice at the appropriate times. It may often require the editing of the work and a combination of storytelling and text-reading.

Editing works

Many works of fiction, particularly novels and other prose works, are written initially for silent readers, who have time to relish a surfeit of words. Yet when we read aloud we change the genre somewhat, in a similar way to Andrew Davies, who adapted *Pride and Prejudice* for television. A good example is Tolkien's *The Hobbit*, a delight to read in its entirety, but which makes for less successful entertainment – as it stands – when read aloud to a class.

Such works require editing, but that editing should maintain the plot with no incidents cut. This is where storytelling becomes a vital tool for the teacher. So, for instance, Chapter 1 'An Unexpected Party' and Chapter 2 'Roast Mutton' would be read in their entirety because they provide dramatic and witty scripts for classroom performance. On the other hand, Chapter 3 'A Short Rest' is less effective in performance as it is overly reflective and explanatory. The full import of its contents, therefore, can successfully be performed through storytelling.[4]

There are obvious dangers in editing. I am reminded of those abridged texts for high school girls – not so very long ago – from which anything remotely sexual was expunged. This emasculated, for instance, most of the works of Shakespeare and Swift and much written before *and* after the nineteenth century! This reign of respectability also saw fairy tales cleansed, particularly of their violence. I reject such editing and argue for cuts purely on the grounds of presentation.

Storytelling and text-reading to present a text

Let us look at the sorts of decisions teachers might make when working out the balance between storytelling and text-reading. At Key Stage 1 the most fruitful direction is to alternate between storytelling whole stories and text-reading whole stories. Most works of fiction for this age group are short and many are in the form of picture books. Children's literacy and story-making abilities are best developed through an equal exposure to storytelling and text-reading with a whole story being presented in one session. This is particularly so in Reception and Year 1. So, perhaps, the teacher tells *Little Red Riding Hood* at one 'sitting' and reads *Where the Wild Things Are* at another. At Year 2, when children generally demand greater depth and length of exposure to storytelling and text-reading, a more episodic approach becomes necessary. Even here, however, most works require little editing.

At Key Stage 2 teachers will gradually feel the need to alternate between storytelling and story-reading when engaged in a single project. The method is essentially flexible and teachers can adapt it to their own personal styles, to the difficulty of the work being presented and to the perceived developmental needs of the children in the class. On the one hand storytelling can be applied to a long novel as a means of shortening the length of the project and provide focus on key aspects of the text. On the other it can assume a greater role in the presentation of texts which are supremely difficult, but extremely valuable to older children. Storytelling can become a sort of fluid tool, enabling ambitious projects to be mounted but making them less formidable. So long as the story itself is psychologically suitable for the children involved no text is beyond consideration when storytelling is used by the teacher to ameliorate its problems.

Developmental criteria for choosing great works

Let us look, for instance, at the possibilities offered by a work of apparently great difficulty, Shakespeare's *King Lear*. When I tackled this great tragedy with a class of Year 5 and Year 6 children I was influenced in my choice by Bruno Bettelheim's book *The Uses of Enchantment*. Discussing the value of fairy stories to the growing child he writes:

> For a story to hold the child's attention, it must entertain him and arouse his curiosity. But to enrich his life, it must stimulate his imagination; help him to develop his intellect and clarify his emotions; be attuned to his anxieties and aspirations; give full recognition to his difficulties, while at the same time suggesting solutions to the problems which perturb him.[5]

So, how does such an argument make *King Lear* relevant to Years 5 and 6 children? A cursory examination of the plot suggests possibilities. A father (Lear) gives away his possessions as rewards for demonstrations of affection, which are false. He is taken in by the blatant pretences of two of his children and punishes the third, who is genuine. Another father (Gloucester) takes sides with one son against the other, after being just as easily conned. Here are examples of something which troubles all children who have brothers of sisters: sibling rivalry. They bear remarkable similarity to the Cinderella and Cain and Abel stories. There are many other relevances, too. A clown (The Fool) continually tests the discipline of his master. People talk about being mad and some are mad. Wickedness and cruelty are seen to triumph and there is an overwhelming sense of unfairness.

Here is a landmark of world literature which is within the psychological grasp of older primary children. According to Bettelheim's criteria it is also a work which offers an outlet for children's deeper disturbances. It is a model for these things and a place to play them out. The Greek word 'catharsis' is relevant here, the 'relief of strong suppressed emotions'. The feeling that 'it's not fair' is, perhaps, the key theme of the play and that is one of childhood's greatest disturbances.

Presenting *King Lear* using storytelling and text-reading

The dilemma when presenting Shakespeare is the language. On the one hand, if the teacher only tells the story, then the children are not really engaging with Shakespeare at all. Shakespeare's stories were not created by him. He lifted them from other sources. The importance of Shakespeare lies in the language. To do Shakespeare with children implies exposing them to Shakespeare's language and here is the other horn of the dilemma: that language is too difficult.

The dilemma is resolved through a dramatic storytelling approach which carries significant extracts of Shakespeare's language. By 'dramatic' I do not mean 'once upon a time there was a King called Lear, who . . .'. This is a play, so, whenever it is performed it is now, the present. The story, therefore, begins with something like 'The scene is a state room in King Lear's palace. King Lear is due to arrive to make an important announcement and two dukes – Kent and Gloucester – are chatting as they wait for him.'[6] This is how the play opens, not with Lear but with these characters, and this is where the storytelling should begin. So that the children would already be familiar with the characters, a poster showing their relationships would be prepared and rehearsed.

So far storytelling has carried the fiction, but soon Shakespeare's language would rise to prominence in this method, the teacher saying, 'A servant brings in a coronet, followed by King Lear, Cornwall, Albany, Goneril, Regan, Cordelia and Attendants. Lear speaks to them. He says: "Meantime, we shall express our darker purpose."'

Here the teacher might comment, 'Notice, children, he uses the word "darker". This means "secret" but, maybe, also, "bad".' Then she would continue the quotation:

> Give me the map there. Know that we have divided
> In three our kingdom; and 'tis our fast intent
> To shake all cares and business from our age,
> Conferring them on younger strengths, while we
> Unburthen'd crawl toward death . . .

Much of this opening speech – with some small cuts – would be spoken
in role. To introduce the replies of the daughters to Lear's question

> Which of you shall we say doth love us most?
> That we our largest bounty may extend. . .[7]

the teacher might say, 'Goneril, the eldest daughter, goes over the top. She says she
loves her father "Dearer than eye-sight, space and liberty" and makes other
exaggerated claims. Poor Cordelia, the youngest, wonders what she will be able to say.
Then it's Regan, the middle daughter's turn. She exaggerates even more, saying that
Goneril "comes too short" and that there are no other joys than being with her father.'

The combination of storytelling and text-reading in a project based on a difficult
work like *King Lear* would consist of about 70 per cent storytelling and 30 per cent
text-reading, varied according to the teacher's judgment about the capabilities of her
children and the length of time available. It is essential, however, to follow the Act and
Scene structure, because this is an important characteristic of this genre of fiction.

Recitation or active reading

The relationship between silent reading and reading aloud is fundamentally important
and goes back to those early experiences children have of listening to a grown up
reading to them. At some stage – the earlier the better – it is essential that children see
the pattern of written words on the page and hear them being 'performed' by another's
voice. This is how 'silent' reading is established, not actually in silence itself, but in
listening to another's voice. An inner voice develops and when we read silently we are
really hearing that inner voice. If a child has little experience of hearing a person
reading and of following the words on the page, that inner voice will be muted.

Gradually, the inner voice will be the child's own voice. Perhaps this is the real
moment when a child has finally learnt to read, not when he can 'bark at print' to prove
something to teacher, but when he hears his own voice when reading silently. This
development will be greatly advanced if children have abundant opportunities to read
aloud or, to put it in performance terms, to recite. They need frequent moments when
alone or with others to rehearse, then perform, a recitation from a script. If this is a
habitual part of school life from the very earliest days, children's silent hearing of that
inner voice will be underscored with hundreds of real examples.

This is recognised to some extent in the NLS Framework. In 'The Termly Objectives'
there are frequent references to 'reading aloud' as a means of consolidating learning,
particularly of sentence level objectives, as in this from Year 2, Term 1: '3. to recognise
and take account of commas and exclamation marks in reading aloud with appropriate
expression'.[8] If children are involved regularly in reciting texts through a process of
rehearsal followed by performance, such an objective will be achieved easily because a
comma and an exclamation mark will be like a note on a page of music, a cue as to
how to speak the sentence. This is active reading, making the sounds yourself
sometimes with other voices, striving to present meaning through the way you speak
the lines and sentences. It is a key way of working, which will open up quick routes to
the acquisition of literacy skills.

Retelling stories

In Chapter 2, I emphasise the importance of the visual in the remembering of storylines. It was Hugh Lupton of 'The Company of Storytellers' who first made me aware of this connection between visualisation in story memory as opposed to learning the words of a story by heart. Hugh had said during a workshop, 'Try to see the pictures then the words will look after themselves.'[9]

The storytellers of old simply learnt their stories from other storytellers and were highly skilled visual memorisers. Modern storytellers, however, are also readers and many of the stories they tell will have been learnt from books. The process for doing this is straightforward but, initially, time-consuming, and is as follows:

1. Read the story once or twice then put it aside.
2. Run through the events out loud to yourself, making a mental note of the parts which are still vague.
3. Read the story again, particularly the vague parts.
4. Go though the main events again out loud.
5. Now try to visualise everything in each scene or picture, right down to the clothes a character might be wearing or what a house or castle actually looks like.
6. Try to visualise the whole story like a silent film.
7. When you can visualise the sequence fairly well, tell the story to someone, being aware of how it sounds.
8. Tell it again and again. By about the third or fourth telling the story is yours.

It is a much easier process in the classroom simply due to the fact that children can work in collaboration, telling and listening to each other as part of their work.

In all fiction work in the classroom, storytelling is a key activity like recitation. It develops memory across the full scale of learning, a keen sense of story structure and narrative fluency. Whether the children are engaging with the entire text of a fiction or with a presentation involving storytelling and text-reading, their understanding and knowledge of the story will be more fully developed if they establish the story initially with others through storytelling. The process should go something like this:

1. Teacher makes her presentation, by reading a whole text, telling a whole story or by combining the two.
2. In pairs or small groups the children consolidate the story by taking turns to tell parts of it and correcting each other in a spirit of collaboration.
3. Pairs or small groups test each other for accuracy of recall.

Such a process will greatly increase children's ability to remember all forms of story if used habitually. It will enable them to understand complex plots at a much earlier age and open up deeper learning of the full range of aspects of fiction: characterisation, the importance of location, the figurative use of language, the interweaving of plots and how they shape and are shaped by the behaviour of the characters. A storytelling process such as this is a key one for developing text level work in reading comprehension and, ultimately, writing composition.

Conferencing

For the learning objectives in the 'Framework' to be realised a more organised use of discussion in necessary. According to the literacy hour structure, part of the 20 minutes section should be spent on group work and to attain such an objective, as 'to discuss the enduring appeal of established authors'[10] requires the full participation of all children. In the past a sort of open forum, led by the teacher and with the children joining in if they had the confidence to do so, was the model for classroom discussion. This, however, only affords talking opportunities to a minority of articulate, willing and self-confident children. No matter how good the teacher is at managing such a forum, there is usually a silent majority.

A better model is available in conferencing, an idea which was developed in the 1980s as a result of The National Oracy Project's work.[11] Its advantages are that it is based on small group discussion with a tighter agenda and maximises the number of real participants in the talk. If used as an habitual activity all the children benefit. They will quickly understand how to do it and that everybody is expected to speak at some, if not all, stages. Conferencing can be effectively started in Year 2 and this is how to do it:

- Divide the class into small groups who are able to work and talk together.
- Each group chooses a scribe to record its ideas and feelings for reporting in a plenary. This job should revolve so that every child does it at some time.
- The children read say, a passage out loud, taking turns and helping each other.
- They look for certain features, depending on the focus identified by the teacher. These features will normally relate to 'text level work', particularly in reading comprehension.
- When they have held their meetings and the scribes have noted the main points, all groups join for a plenary in which the scribes present the groups' ideas.
- The teacher attempts a summary, adding her own ideas.

Used regularly, as a means of exploring meaning in fiction, conferencing can develop in children the self-confidence and ability to form opinions and offer them to others. If they work in groups of trusted peers, the pressure is taken off the quieter, less articulate children so that they can develop the range of reflective and analytical skills necessary to make progress as readers and writers of fiction.

Composing stories

It is often said that nobody ever really composes an original story, that there are a relatively small number of plots and that all stories are variations of them. To a certain extent it is difficult to disagree with this claim and it would, therefore, appear that the art of story-making depends on how these plots are developed, how the characters are made to interact with each other and with their surroundings. If this is accepted it makes the composition of stories in primary schools more straightforward. It makes the tales children hear and read of great value for their development as makers of stories themselves.

As we have seen in Chapter 2, the storytellers of old did not invent their own stories, they inherited them and their originality was found in the way they told them. Their art was, quite literally, in the telling. Many playwrights, story writers and novelists have also been quite prepared to remake rather than create their plots. Shakespeare is an obvious example, but most writers rework stories, both from real life and other sources.

We should, therefore, feel no inhibitions in our primary classrooms about children retelling or rewriting stories they have heard or read. However, they should be encouraged to use their own words, to be prepared to add to the story, embellish it, introduce digressions, personal observations and turns of phrase. It is from these ways of appropriating stories that their personal style will develop. However, most children are unwilling to remain inside the stories of others. In order to develop fully as writers they need to assemble their own plots, invent their own characters, create locations and follow themes. In short, they regularly need the sense of control over the various strands of material that go to make a good yarn and they need this control when storytelling and when story-writing. A range of opportunities is therefore required which involves all children as storytellers and story-writers. Ideally, such a range would include the retelling and rewriting of those that are read and heard, and the telling and writing of those that are invented by the children.

Dance and drama

To a large extent the reading aloud or recitation of a fictional text becomes a form of drama. However simple and unrehearsed it may be, it is a performance. If we bring expression into our voices when reading the description of a character, place or object, in a sense we are providing costumes and make up, set and properties for the performance. When we differentiate between the voices of different characters we go into role. These dramatic elements are even more in evidence when we tell the story, because the freedom from holding a book enables us to establish eye-contact with the audience, increase our gestures and move about like characters. This will, however, have far greater power for children if they take their activity a stage further into role-play and improvisation. For instance, Bilbo's panic during 'The Unexpected Party' becomes more rooted in a child's awareness and memory if he or she has pretended to be Bilbo.[12]

Dance and drama offer a range of ways of re-enacting fiction, from the realistic portrayal of a scene in a story using the actual words of characters to the exploration of a theme in a more symbolic way. There is a continuum of dramatic activity and each element is valuable in activating a story and its meanings.

Speaking the words of characters

Throughout all work with fiction, whether storytelling or text-reading, children should tell or read a character's words in a different way from those of the narrative. Constant emphasis on this differentiation will develop children's ideas of characterisation, emphasise the distinction between direct and reported speech and make it easy for them to understand how playscripts work.

Making tableaux vivants (living pictures) and miming

Descriptions of characters, both as individuals and in groups can be interpreted by the children through a process of reassembling the description. This involves facial expression, postures and the physical relationships between a group of characters in a scene. A natural progression is to make the still pictures change position, leading into mime. For this latter to be fully realised a language of gestures has to be established by all the participants. For instance, to show one character being afraid of another, the child might move into a position which is lower and move a forearm across the face, accompanied by an appropriate facial expression.

Dance drama

This differs somewhat from mime because here movements are freer and usually more symbolic. Gestures are more sweeping and flowing and there is less need to develop an agreed language of gestures.

Role-play, using improvised dialogue and gesture

This literally means making words and movements up as you go along. It extends storytelling into physical actions involving the individual becoming the character rather than merely speaking the character's words.

Role-play, using invented written dialogue or dialogue taken from text

This is a refinement of the improvisational process and involves a written text, either made up by the children or taken from the written story. This sometimes presents difficulties to younger children, particularly during the rehearsal stage of development.

Scripted plays

The logical development for the use of pieces of written dialogue is the fully scripted play, and the best way of starting this important work is to make a play for voices or a radio play. Children need to learn the correct conventions for writing such scripts, which is as follows:

- Decide on the piece of text to be used. In a novel a chapter is a useful unit. Establish who the characters are and which are their words. If any speeches are too long they need to be cut. Create a character or characters called 'Narrator'. If more than one is to be used call them 'First Narrator', 'Second Narrator' and so on.
- When writing the script put the character's name on the left with the words spoken immediately after it like this:
  Danny: Where did you go, Dad?
  Dad: You must be tired out.
  Danny: I'm not a bit tired. Couldn't we light the lamp for a little while?
  Narrator: My father put a match to the wick of the lamp.
  Dad: How about a hot drink?
- The children need to realise that phrases such as 'said Danny' are no longer needed.

- Instructions for sound effects or the movements of the character to be written in italic in brackets.[13]

Enactments in dance and drama are invaluable mediums through which children can bring stories to life by embodying them. The embodiment of new learning makes it more memorable and permanent for children.

Art and music

The use of these two art forms can illuminate meaning in fiction and be used to develop personal response. They offer unique ways of exploring and celebrating the other worlds in stories, one visually, the other aurally. With drama and dance they have also been ways of enacting the great stories of all cultures throughout history. In the enactment of Black Elk's power vision, signs and symbols are painted on the teepee and the horses and new songs are taught and performed.

Stories have always been a source of inspiration for artists and musicians. In art the precedent was set as far back as the cave artists who told the story of the hunt on cave walls, and this precedent has been followed by many artists in most art movements. Similarly in music; tunes were made for dances based on myths, and songs were sung, traditions which have remained strong, most obviously in ballet and opera.

Using art

Portraits of characters

These can be made with any media, including the three-dimensional. If the children use descriptions in the text as a basis for making portraits, this helps develop comprehension of the material. It also creates a more focused portrait. The children need to try to reveal a character's attitudes as well as physical descriptions in their portraits. The background to a portrait offers further opportunties for developing the persona of a character.

Landscapes and settings

Any media can also be used to develop visual and tactile responses to descriptions of places and settings in a piece of fiction. Again, the text provides the clues and stimuli for this work.

Abstract and semi-abstract work

A valuable way of drawing children's attention to the figurative use of language is to set the children the task of realising a metaphor, simile or other kind of visual image in a drawing, painting, sculpture or other piece of art. This is a fruitful way of exploring the deeper levels of any work.

Use of artists' works

Any work in art can be enhanced if children study works by the artists. For instance, in Oscar Wilde's *The Selfish Giant*[14], art work on the giant's garden benefits if the children study paintings of gardens in general and those of the impressionists in particular.

Using music

Sound effects

The simplest form of musical response to fiction is the making of sounds to represent incidents: e.g. a character arrives at a house and a knocking sound is made. This can be developed further and is particularly valuable in plays for voices.

Signature tunes

Prokofiev's 'Peter and the Wolf' is an example of the simple tune being used to represent a character. Every time a character enters, the tune plays so that the audience begins to associate the one with the other. Such tunes are very easy to compose. A giant, for instance, can be represented with a simple pattern of loud percussion sounds, a fairy with a pattern of dainty, high sounds.

Tone poems

Sound effects can be developed beyond the literal, knock-represents-someone-coming type of effect. The children can be challenged to make motifs and patterns to capture the mood of a scene in a story. Usually, a good range of instruments, including tuned ones, is required for successful work of this kind.

Making songs

Any group of words with a clear rhythm can be set to music and lead to the making of a song. The basic process is simple: the children recite the words, clapping an accompaniment; transfer the rhythm onto a group of chime bars, glockenspiel or xylophone; when they have found a tune they try to sing it; they rehearse this, then record it in some way.

Using composers' works

When making the various kinds of plays identified above, mood and atmosphere can be created by playing recorded music rather than sound effects or tone poems which the children have composed themselves. The process of selection is valuable both for understanding a text and for developing musical perception.

Art and music elevate stories, bringing certain key elements into the foreground. They offer other, different and very practical ways of consolidating literacy. When children make art or music in response to stories, they make them memorable because of the visual and aural impacts on imagination brought by these ways of working. They also help to make the experience of story enjoyable and thereby strengthen their attitude towards books.

Presenting finished work

A vital means of coming to an understanding of the world is the making of stories in the mind. In his book *The Meaning Makers* Gordon Wells calls this 'storying' and claims that it is 'one of the most fundamental means of making meaning and, as such, it is an activity that pervades all aspects of learning'.[15] This inner storymaking, however, often demands outward expression, and children's sense of audience for the sharing of stories is well developed. From an early age most children seek to join in when anecdotes are exchanged. Telling stories to a sympathetic audience is something children need to do for personal and social reasons. Wells argues that, when children tell their stories, they express their own interpretation of ideas and events. This use of an audience, according to Wells, provides 'a cultural interpretation of those aspects of human experience that are of fundamental and abiding concern'.[16] It is a way of being inducted into a culture and of being valued by it. As children tell their own anecdotes and stories they naturally use materials from those which they have learnt from others and follow structures which give the tales significance.

If Wells is right, the presentation of children's work in relation to fiction takes on a greatly enhanced importance in a school. If ordinary, everyday story exchanges are important cultural events, then the more formal occasions assume very high status. So, the ten minute plenary at the end of a literacy hour is insufficient and should be supplemented by a more formal, greater event at the end of a unit of fiction work. It should be more akin to a celebration of progress in which stories are told and read, paintings displayed, plays and dances enacted, some to music composed by the children. Such events would also involve the publication of children's own stories in small editions of multiple copies for distribution to interested people. This is how a sense of audience will be developed, through making the idea of audience prominent in the school. This raises literacy from a strategy with targets into a life-enriching experience.

References

1. Hughes, T. (1976) 'Myth and Education', in Fox, G. *et al.* (eds), *Writers, Critics and Children*, 81. London: William Heinemann.
2. Gadamer, H-G. (1986) *The Relevance of the Beautiful*, 111. Cambridge: Cambridge University Press.
3. Coleridge, S. T. (1963) 'The Rime of the Ancient Mariner', in *Poems*. London: Dent Dutton.
4. Tolkien, J. R. R. (1937) *The Hobbit*. London: George Allen and Unwin.
5. Bettelheim, B. (1976) *The Uses of Enchantment*, 5. London: Thames and Hudson.
6. Shakespeare, W. (1964) *King Lear*, Act 1, Scene 1. London: Methuen Publishers.
7. *King Lear*, Act 1, Scene 2.
8. Stannard, J. (1998) *National Literacy Strategy Framework for Teaching*. 26. London: Department for Education and Employment.
9. Lupton, H. (1988) Workshop in Clwyd.
10. Stannard, J. (1998) 26.
11. See Norman, K. (ed.) (1992) *Thinking Voices*. London: Hodder & Stoughton.
12. Tolkien (1937).
13. Dahl, R. (1975) *Danny the Champion of the World*. London: Jonathan Cape Publications.
14. Wilde, O. (1962) 'The Selfish Giant', in *The Happy Prince and Other Stories*. Harmondsworth: Puffin Books.
15. Wells, G. (1986) *The Meaning Makers*, 194. London: Hodder & Stoughton.
16. Wells (1986) 195.

Chapter Four

Exploring oral traditions

Oral traditions

Oral culture can be defined as 'culture without writing' and it is sometimes assumed that oral culture was gradually replaced by culture with writing or 'literary culture'. It seems obvious that the book replaced the spoken story as the main source of information, belief, song and story and the chief means of educating people. However, as Goody argues, 'Writing does not supplant oral communication; it is merely another channel of communication, substituting for the oral only in certain contexts but at the same time developing new ones.'[1]

The rise of alphabets and the printing press did change the role of oral communication in the development of culture. Goody continues:

> Oral communication in societies with writing is not the same as it is in those without it. In the latter the oral tradition has to bear all the burden of cultural transmission. In literate societies, however, the oral tradition is vested with only part of the total body of literary activity, of standardised verbal forms.[2]

The recent revival of storytelling to become a popular form of entertainment in its own right suggests it was not so much replaced in our culture as neglected. With the rediscovery of storytelling has come the realisation of its educational value. The storytellers of the oral cultures, who carried, to use Goody's phrase, 'all the burden of cultural transmission', not only developed prodigious memories but also great mental agility in adapting their stories to each audience. These abilities are as valuable in contemporary society as ever they were. Indeed, a modern economy, more dependent on services than manufacturing, requires people with flexible minds, long memories and quick recall, who can adapt quickly. Most of all it needs articulate people, who can tell stories in the broadest sense. So, strangely, many of the bases of oral culture are necessary again.

Although stories from various oral cultures are now passed on to us by means of the book, most still carry the verbal structures that make them ideal models for developing storytelling. In other words, by using stories derived from the oral culture we provide children with ideal material for developing their storytelling skills in particular and their speaking and listening skills in general. Stories from oral culture have a directness of voice because they are closer to actual speech. Some are virtually transcriptions of speech. When the brothers Grimm, for instance, travelled the German-speaking world, their 'aim was to preserve the *marchen* in the form in which they were still being told in the German provinces'. They said:

> As for our method of collecting, our primary concern has been for accuracy and truth. We have added nothing of our own, nor have we embellished any incident or feature of the tale, but we have rendered the content just as we received it.[3]

If it is true that fairy and folk tales, myths and legends provide ideal 'training grounds' for storytelling and oracy the implication is that works need to be chosen which are as close to transcriptions of speech as possible. Many translations do fulfil this, but there are many eighteenth and nineteenth century versions which are contaminated by implanted moralistic attitudes. Jack Zipes claims that many writers actually manipulated stories to suit the agenda of their times. As the 'literary fairy tale for children', he writes, '. . . began to constitute itself as a genre, [it] became more an institutionalised discourse with manipulation as one of its components.'[4] As far as language structures and style are concerned a similar problem exists with the myths. The best sources of the Greek myths are to be found in the verse translations of Homer rather than in the prose translations aimed at children. This was why Robert Fitzgerald was used in Clwyd's 'The Odyssey Project' of 1987.[5]

Making choices, however, is always a compromise. No written version of a story from the oral tradition is going to be like the real thing. This is a compromise I have had to make in retelling the stories for literacy hour lessons later in this chapter. I have assumed the role of a storyteller when writing the tales. In doing so I have tried to hear a voice in my head, but am aware that this is only a simulation of the real thing. In one sense, however, this hardly matters, because the written down oral story is only in a temporary state of fixedness so long as it is subsequently retold. Once a storyteller has learnt a story from its written text he or she will begin to change it. This is one of the liberating features that oral stories have, as Propp argues: 'If the reader of a work of literature is a powerless censor and critic devoid of authority, anyone listening to folklore is a potential future performer, who, in turn, consciously or unconsciously, will introduce changes into the work.'[6]

This points to a further educational value in engaging primary children in telling stories from the oral tradition. It is an empowering activity, which not only connects them to the roots of their own and other cultures, but also allows them opportunities to reshape material to suit their own situations.

Fairy and folk tales

If children participate in listening to and telling stories from the fairy and folk traditions there are, according to Bettelheim, significant psychological and emotional benefits available to them. Bettelheim argues that this genre in particular offers assistance in dealing with the various problems associated with growing up and in the development of self-value and responsibility. Any child, he claims, 'needs to understand what is going on within his conscious self so that he can also cope with that which goes on in his subconscious'. But this is achieved '. . . not through rational comprehension of the nature and content of his unconscious, but by becoming familiar with it through spinning out daydreams – ruminating, rearranging, and fantasising about suitable story elements in response to unconscious pressures.'[7]

For Bettelheim fairy tales are particularly well placed in this respect

> . . . because they offer new dimensions to the child's imagination which would be impossible for him to discover as truly on his own. Even more important, the form and structure of fairy tales suggest images to the child by which he can structure his daydreams and with them give better direction to his life.[8]

Although a writer such as Zipes may argue that fairy and folk tales 'are not the best therapy in the world for children'[9] Bettelheim makes out a convincing case for this kind of use. His argument is validated by the fact that, as a child psychologist himself, he helped many children to deal with their psychological disorders by using fairy tales as part of the therapy. His choice of fairy tales for this kind of work was made because the fairy tale '. . . simplifies all situations. Its figures are clearly drawn; and details, unless very important, are eliminated. All characters are typical rather than unique.'[10]

By such means children find representation of key fears and emotions. For instance, the fear of the death of a parent is given substance in the figure of the wicked stepmother, a familiar character in fairy tales. Similarly, the young child's feeling of powerlessness is made manifest in the hopeless youngest son – sometimes a daughter – a character common throughout all cultures. In every story this hopeless child proves to be the best in the end, overcoming the most impossible of odds to gain their victory.

Fairy and folk tales present characters with whom it is easy to identify or to reject. The good character is simply presented without ambiguity. Children can, therefore, quickly take on that role in their imaginations, as Bettelheim argues, 'not because of his goodness, but because the hero's condition makes a deep, positive appeal . . .'[11] Through such simplicity in the presentation of characters, themes and situations a whole range of fears, anxieties, hopes and wishes are embodied for children. They can, therefore, play these things out in their imaginations safely. If, in addition, children engage with the fairy and folk genre as storytellers they assume powers over the material which adds a further dimension to its value.

Myths and legends

Bettelheim argues that fairy tales are more appropriate than myths for use with children, mainly because they present an optimistic outlook on life, a view supported by Zipes. Good characters 'live happily ever after', when they have seen off horrendous odds against them. Good triumphs over evil and, if all seems hopeless, there is always magic to transform it! Myths, on the other hand, usually end tragically and often unfairly. The gods play with the mortals and a single act of vanity or aggression can end in the annihilation not only of the perpetrator but also of his or her entire family or kin. As Bettelheim argues,

> The myth is pessimistic, while the fairy story is optimistic, no matter how terrifyingly serious some features of the story may be. It is this decisive difference which sets the fairy tale apart from other stories in which equally fantastic events occur . . .[12]

There is another fundamental difference between fairy tales and myths, which Bettelheim claims as reason enough to rely solely on fairy tales in our work with children. This is that, however fantastic the events might be, there is a sense that many of the heroes could be you or me. In myths all events and the actions of the heroes are, to use Bettelheim's words, 'absolutely unique' and 'could not have happened . . . in any other setting'. The events are 'awe-inspiring and could not possibly happen to an ordinary mortal'. On the other hand, he claims that in fairy tales even the most remarkable encounters are related in casual, everyday ways.'[13]

To a great extent Bettelheim's argument here is spurious. Children need to engage with both genres of oral fiction. There is a confusion in Bettelheim's notion of the hero. Such a person, for instance, in Greek mythology is not a mortal or a god, but, rather the offspring of the two. Often this happens when Zeus comes to earth in disguise and seduces a beautiful mortal woman. So, for instance, Perseus is born human but with supernatural powers. Throughout his story there is a sense that he will be protected through the intervention of a god under instructions from Zeus himself. The fairy tale hero is a mortal, who is helped by fairy magic because he or she shows virtue. Thus the youngest son, instead of rejecting or being rude to the old man during the journey, helps him and is rewarded.

Now children will identify with both types of hero, but in different ways. The mythical one is awesome to the child, is a star in the galaxy to be admired at something of a distance, whereas the one in fairy and folk tales is him or herself with extra added on. The mythical hero is beyond the child. The fairy tale hero could be the child in fantasy. Both kinds are necessary to children, particularly as they grow older. This is a crucial point. Few teachers would introduce four-year-olds to Odysseus, but five or six years later his exploits would be wondrous.

Bettelheim and Zipes exaggerate the effects of tragedy on children. It is a patronising attitude to suggest that they cannot experience *catharsis* (relief of strong, suppressed emotions) which is the purpose of tragedy in literature, or the feeling of 'there but for the grace of God go I'. Children, particularly older children, are fully capable of handling tragedy. When their identification with the hero is one of admiration from a distance, tragedy is part of that distant playing out. They will easily accept that as part of the fate of heroes in such stories, whereas they might feel cast down by a tragic ending, say, for Cinderella or Jack.

The legend occupies an interesting position somewhere between history and mythology. There is always the sense in a legend that much of it might have been historically true, yet so much of it is also fantastic. There is the sense with a legend that it is set in a particular time and place. Robin Hood in Sherwood Forest at the time when Richard the Lionheart was away fighting in the Crusades and England was ruled by his wicked brother John is a typical legend. The relationship with history is fascinating, none more so than the legend of King Arthur and Camelot, which still inspires archaeological digs for evidence.

Heroes in legends are mortal and generally their exploits are not guided by a supernatural force but rather by their own virtues. The exploits of King Arthur are different in this respect as magic rests with Merlin and, later, tragically with Morgan la Fay. There is a sense in which the making of legends is always with us and this offers great opportunities for children as makers of stories. Who is a local hero? What stories are there about that person? How have those stories developed? How could they be developed further? These are questions which may lead to active, living legends being created in classrooms.

Literacy strategy lessons

In the following sections I retell fairy and folk stories from a range of different cultures: Africa, China, Eastern Europe, Scandinavia, Iran, Armenia and Russia. As they listen, retell and work through the suggested literacy and other activities, children may see that, whatever the cultural background of the story, the same dilemmas occur and are met with the same combination of courage and cleverness by heroes.

The suggested activities are intended as action plans for the celebration of the stories and for literacy hour work. Each set of notes follows the range of work statements in the Framework and the appropriate Termly Objectives for word level, sentence level and text level work. There are also activities in the arts, which are vital to the approaches being promoted in this book. Every story should be introduced in the following way:

- Make a large poster version – in several pages.
- Read and/or tell the story to the children, inviting them to join in with repetitions as appropriate.
- Establish that they remember it by going over the main points through questioning.
- Ask them in pairs or groups to retell the story with the listeners making corrections.
- Briefly recap the story at the start of each session.
- Tell the children which country or continent the story is from and something about it.

Work based on every story should conclude with the following kinds of plenary or sharing:

- Frequent revision of word work items with regular chanting of the sounds.
- Children to practise retelling the story in their own words and reading parts of it, paying due attention to punctuation.
- Plays and dances to be rehearsed and performed to audiences, sometimes invited from other classes. Musical pieces to be performed as part of these occasions.
- Art to be exhibited in classroom or corridor galleries.
- Writing to be anthologised and put on display.

YR: T3. 'Why do monkeys live in trees'?

Text

Long ago there was a panther who was not very clever. This is what happened.

Panther went hunting but did not catch any dinner. Not a thing did he catch. Panther was tired. Panther was hungry. But worst of all Panther was itchy. All over Panther's coat there were fleas. Itchy, jumpy fleas. They drove Panther mad.

Panther ran round and round trying to catch the fleas. Not a flea did he catch. Not one. Panther was tired. Panther was hungry. But worst of all Panther was itchy.

Just then Panther saw Monkey passing quickly by. 'Monkey,' he shouted, 'Please pick out my fleas. Please!' Now Panther and Monkey were friends so Monkey picked out Panther's fleas, one by itchy one.

Do you know how nice it is to have your fleas picked out? Panther liked it. He fell fast asleep. But as you also know, monkeys like to play tricks. So, as soon as Panther was asleep Monkey tied his tail to a tree. Yes, a tree!

Poor Panther! When he woke up he could not get up. His tail was tied to a tree. Yes, a tree! Panther pulled. Panther tugged. Panther waggled his bottom. He could not get his tail free. Just then Panther saw Snail passing slowly by. 'Snail,' he shouted. 'Please undo my tail. Please Snail!' Panther and Snail were friends so Snail untied Panther's tail.

'Thank you,' said Panther and ran home. But he wanted to get his own back on Monkey. So Panther told his friend Gorilla that in three days' time he would lie down dead in front of his lair.

Gorilla told the birds that in three days' time Panther would lie down dead in front of his lair.

They told the animals that in three days' time Panther would lie down dead in front of his lair.

Three days passed by.

Panther went and lay down dead in front of his lair.

Gorilla came to see Panther lying dead.

The birds came to see Panther lying dead.

The animals came to see Panther lying dead.

Snail came to see Panther lying dead.

Monkey came to see Panther lying dead.

Suddenly, Panther jumped up and tried to catch Monkey. He missed, of course, because Panther was not very clever.

Monkey jumped up into a tree. That is why monkeys live in trees. They are frightened that Panthers might catch them.

Word and sentence

- Make a chart of the letters of the alphabet in large and small case.
- Find a picture with jungle animals on it and put it in the 'Aa' space with the word 'Animals' next to it. Repeat for Panther, Fleas, Monkey, Snail, Gorilla and birds.
- Talk through this chart every day, getting the children to chant the names each time. Ask them for animals to fill the other spaces.
- Have animal names ready in case the children can't think of any.
- If you are left with x to fill add Xiphias, a kind of swordfish, to the chart.
- Keep refining the children's chanting of names and initial letters.
- Pick out simple sentences and write in big letters onto strips of paper for the wall. Good examples are: 'Panther was tired.', 'Panther was hungry.' and 'Panther liked it'.
- For each sentence children to say what was happening or what happened next.
- Point out the capital 'P' for Panther and say why it is there.
- Write 'Three days went by.' and ask the children what went before the three days and what comes after them. Point out the capital 'T' for 'Three' and say why it is there.

Reading and writing

Children to:

- Draw animal pictures for the alphabet chart and copy the names onto them.
- Draw pictures of scenes in the story and say what they show, to be scribed for them to copy.
- Play word recognition games with the names of the animals of the alphabet chart.
- Retell the story in their own words to their group with other members saying whether it is right or not.

Dance and drama

- In the school hall children to re-enact the story.
- Ask them to make these different animals:
  1. favourite pets at home
  2. wild ones such as elephants or giraffes
  3. animals in the story: Panther, Monkey, Snail and Gorilla.
- Refine their movements by using descriptive words in the story (e.g. 'tired' Panther, 'itchy' Panther, Panther with his tail tied to a tree and Panther 'lying dead').
- In pairs, children to re-enact encounters between Panther and Monkey, Panther and Snail and Panther and Gorilla.
- Play passing the message 'In three days' time Panther will lie down dead in front of his lair.'
- Choose one child for Panther and ask the others to look at him 'lying dead in front of his lair' and one as Monkey. Re-enact Panther trying to catch Monkey.

Art

- Show the children pictures of different African animals.
- Ask them to choose their favourites, ensuring that Panther, Monkey, Snail and Gorilla are represented.
- Hide the pictures and invite the children to paint their animals in a jungle setting.

Y1: T1. 'The Nung Gwama'

Text

In the olden days in China there was a poor widow who had no children. But she had her old mother and father who lived in the town. One day she made some cakes for them and walked to the town. As she passed a bamboo hedge out jumped the Nung Gwama, shouting:

> 'Sniff, sniff! I smell a snack.
> I'll chew your legs. I'll crunch your back.'

Now the Nung Gwama is horrible. His body is like a muddy bull. His head is as big as a kitchen sink. He shows his dirty teeth. He shakes his sharp claws. Flop, flop go his feet. The smell is of cabbages and he shouts:

'Sniff, sniff! I smell a snack.
I'll chew your legs. I'll crunch your back.'

He said to the poor widow, 'Give me those cakes.' She fell on her knees and started crying, 'I can't. They're for my mother and father.'

The Nung Gwama said, 'Keep your cakes. Tonight I will come to your door and shout:

Sniff, sniff! I smell a snack.
I'll chew your legs. I'll crunch your back.

Then I will tear you to bits with my sharp claws and I will munch you up with my dirty teeth.' The poor widow was scared stiff and howled,

'Wah! Wah! What can I do?
Nung Gwama's coming! What can I do?'

The Nung Gwama flopped away, leaving a smell of cabbages. The poor widow sat down at the side of the road.

A farmer spreading cow muck on his field, stopped and came to her. 'What is the matter?' he asked. The poor widow howled:

'Wah! Wah! What can I do?
Nung Gwama's coming! What can I do?'

The farmer gave her some cow muck and said, 'Spread it over your front door. It might put Nung Gwama off.' She thanked him but still she howled.

Next came a man selling snakes. He stopped and came to her. He asked what was the matter. Again she howled,

'Wah! Wah! What can I do?
Nung Gwama's coming! What can I do?'

The Snake Man saw the bag of cow muck. He had heard the farmer say it was for spreading on her front door to upset Nung Gwama. He gave her two snakes and said, 'Put these in your water jar. Nung Gwama will try to wash the cow muck off his hands and the snakes will sting him.' She thanked him but still she howled.

Next came a man selling biting fish. He stopped and came to her. He asked what was the matter. Again she howled:

'Wah! Wah! What can I do?
Nung Gwama's coming! What can I do?'

The Fish Man saw the two snakes in the bag. He had heard the Snake Man say they were for stinging Nung Gwama on the hands. He gave her two biting fish and said, 'Put these in your cooking pot. When Nung Gwama is stung by the snakes he will want to bathe his hands in warm water. The fish will bite him.' She thanked him but still she howled.

Next came a man selling eggs. He stopped and came to her. He asked what was the matter? Again she howled:

'Wah! Wah! What can I do?
Nung Gwama's coming! What can I do?'

The Egg Man saw the two fish in a bucket. He had heard the Fish Man say they were for biting Nung Gwama on the hands. He gave her some eggs and said, 'Put these eggs in the ashes of your fire. When Nung Gwama is bitten by the fish his hands will bleed. He will use the ash to stop the blood. The eggs will blow up in his face.' She thanked him but still she howled.

Next came a man with big stones on a cart. He stopped and came to her. He asked what was the matter. Again she howled:

'Wah! Wah! What can I do?
Nung Gwama's coming! What can I do?'

The Big Stone Man looked at the things the poor widow had been given. He gave her a big stone and said, 'Tie this big stone on a rope from your roof beam. When Nung Gwama comes to get you, cut the rope and the stone will hit him on the head. Then finish him off with this iron bar.' She thanked him, borrowed a cart and took all her gifts home.

Back at home the poor widow put cow muck over her front door, the snakes in the water jar, the biting fish in the cooking pot, the eggs in the ashes of the fire. She hung the big stone from the roof beam. Then she got into bed and waited for Nung Gwama to come.

When darkness came so did he, shouting:

'Sniff, sniff! I smell a snack.
I'll chew your legs. I'll crunch your back.'

Nung Gwama banged down the front door and shouted, 'Eeeee! That's disgusting! It stinks! I must get some water.'

He put his hands into the water jar and shouted, 'Ow! Snakes! I must get some warm water.' He put his hands into the cooking pot and shouted, 'Ow! Biting fish! I must get some ashes.'

He put his hands into the ashes and shouted, 'Ow! What's that? I can't see.'

He stumbled under the big stone. The poor widow cut the rope and down it came. This time the Nung Gwama shouted, 'Aaaaa! Aaaaa!' His head was flattened. The poor widow got the iron bar. She shouted, 'Take that you nasty beast! And that! And that!'

And that was the end of Nung Gwama. The people of the village thanked the poor widow. She took the cakes to her mother and father and they had a party.

Word and sentence

- List *-ing* words: 'shouting', 'crying', 'leaving'. Ask children who is 'shouting' (Nung Gwama), who is 'crying' (Poor Widow) and what Nung Gwama is 'leaving' (smell of cabbages). Write these opposite the words to establish the link between *-ing* words and ideas in the story.
- Can the children find some more? What ideas are they for? Add to list.
- Repeat with words ending *-ff* ('sniff', 'stiff', 'off'), *-ll* ('bull', 'still', 'will') and *-ck* ('snack', 'back').
- List *sh-* and *ch-* words: 'she', 'shows', 'shouted'; 'China', 'children', 'chew'.
- Look for words with capital letters and look for full stops. Highlight in bright colours.

Reading

- Children to tell the story in turns in their groups, the others checking for accuracy.
- Point out the differences between their spoken versions and the written one, e.g. they miss out details such as 'She fell on her knees and started crying', more likely saying, 'She cried'.
- Divide the text between the groups. Children to find – with help – the 'special story language', e.g. 'He said to the poor widow'. Children to copy these out.
- Children to decide in their groups what kind of people the characters in the story are in 'appearance', 'behaviour', 'attitudes'.
- Draw their attention to phrases which start, continue and end the story: e.g.'In the olden days', 'Next came a man selling . . .'.
- Children to learn the Nung Gwama's and the Poor Widow's shouts.

Writing

- Each child to make a simple drawing of the Poor Widow meeting one of the characters.
- Ensure equal numbers of each picture to make sets for shuffling and sorting into order.
- Each child to specialise in one character and make a drawing with captions to show the appearance, behaviour and attitudes of the character.
- In groups the children to make up the story of 'What else did Nung Gwama do to make everybody afraid of him?'

Dance and drama

- Children to move like the characters.
- Ask questions such as 'How would the Egg Man carry his eggs?', 'How would the farmer carry his cow muck?' and so on.
- In pairs children to enact Poor Widow's encounter with Nung Gwama, using the words from the text for the shouts, their own words for the rest.
- If successful divide the class into larger groups, aiming for each one to re-enact the whole story, using their own words, except for the two shouts.

Music

- Use clapping and percussion to emphasise the Nung Gwama jumping out on the Poor Widow.
- Develop this into more rhythmic clapping and percussion for the Nung Gwama's shout. If successful, develop rhythmic claps and percussion for the Poor Widow's shout.

Y2: T2. 'The boy who disappeared'

Text

Once upon a time there was a lord who lived with his lady in a castle in a beautiful valley in Bohemia. On the night before his son was born this lord dreamed that the boy must never touch the ground until his tenth birthday or else something bad would happen.

When the baby was born the lord had all kinds of prams and buggies made to keep him off the ground. Wherever he went a nurse went with him so he was never on his own. It was so boring but he never touched the ground until the day before his tenth birthday. A troupe of actors arrived with the noise of trumpets and cheering down in the courtyard. One of the nurses, who was new, rushed to the window. Just as she looked out she remembered the boy, but it was too late. He was gone.

The lord had the castle searched from top to bottom. But there was no sign of the boy. Search parties were sent to all parts of the lord's lands, to the highest mountain peaks and the deepest caverns. Still there was no sign of the boy. The lord and lady were out of their minds with worry.

Some time later there was news of strange goings on in one of the big rooms of the castle. At midnight footsteps were heard along a passage, followed by moaning and sighing. The lord wanted to find out what this was, but how could he? Nobody wanted to go in the big room at midnight. It was too scary. So the lord offered 300 gold coins to anyone who would spend the night in there.

Many tried and failed. The footsteps and moaning were so weird that everyone who went in soon ran out. Eventually the news came to an old widow who lived with her two daughters in the forest. They were so poor they could hardly feed themselves. What were a few spooky hours to them? The old widow came to the castle and offered to stay all night in the big room. But she asked for lots of things. She asked for pots and pans, crockery and cutlery, food to cook, logs for the fire and a comfy bed with soft sheets and blankets.

Everything she asked for was brought. She made a big fire. Over the fire she hung a pot and started to cook up a casserole. She laid a table with crisp linen and a knife, fork and spoon. The clock struck midnight and she sat down to dine. Then footsteps shuffled into the room and a voice started moaning. The old widow looked round and saw the boy looking as white as ashes. He came to her and said, 'Who are you cooking supper for?'

The old widow replied, 'I'm cooking for myself.' The boy's face dropped and he sighed. He said, 'Who is the table laid for?' The old widow replied, 'It is laid for me, of course.' The boy's face dropped and he moaned. He said, 'Who is the bed made up for?' The old widow replied, 'It is made up for me.' Tears came into the boy's eyes. He turned and left the room moaning. After sleeping the widow went to the lord, told him what happened, took her 300 golden coins and went home.

This was too good to be true for the poor family in the forest. So, after a few weeks, the older daughter came to the castle and offered to spend the night in the big room. Everything was as before. The older daughter ordered all the stuff, lit a fire, cooked supper, laid the table, made the bed. The boy shuffled and moaned in at midnight, asked the same questions and got the same answers. She got her money next morning and left.

By now the poor family was richer and there was another daughter. Soon she, too, was sent to the castle. All seemed as it was before. Midnight came. The fire glowed in the grate, the food cooked in the pot, the table was laid for one and the bed made. The boy shuffled in not expecting much. He said to the younger daughter, who was sweet and kind, 'Who are you cooking supper for?' She replied, 'I was cooking for myself, but there's plenty for both of us.' The boy's face lit up. He asked, 'Who is the table laid for?' The sweet younger daughter replied, 'I did lay it just for me, but it would be nice if you joined me.' The young boy smiled! He asked his third question, 'Who is that bed made for?' The kind younger daughter replied, 'It was made just for me, but it's big enough for two.' The boy smiled again and said, 'Please wait, I must say goodbye to a few friends.'

A great hole opened in the floor and spring air flowed up from it. The boy went down the hole. The girl followed. They landed softly in a beautiful country and the boy walked across a meadow and into a wood made of gold. As he entered all the birds flew around him singing their songs of goodbye. 'Goodbye, my little singing friends,' he replied. The girl was amazed. She broke off a tiny golden twig as a keepsake.

The boy left the golden wood, crossed another meadow and entered a silver wood. As he entered, all the animals ran nuzzling up to him, saying goodbye. 'Goodbye, my gentle friends,' he replied. The girl was amazed by what she saw. She broke off one silver leaf as a keepsake.

Soon they were rushing back up to the big room in the castle and sitting down to supper. They talked for hours without stopping until the boy yawned, cleared away the dishes, got into the bed and fell fast asleep. The girl put a few logs on the fire, got into the bed and soon fell fast asleep.

Late next morning the lord and lady were worried. The girl had not come to them with her news. They went to the big room and knocked on the door. There was no answer. The lord opened the door and saw a wonderful sight – his dear son fast asleep and the girl beside him. How happy everybody was when they sat down to lunch that day! Better still, the boy who disappeared and the girl who saved him with her kindness fell in love and were married some years later. They lived happily ever after.

Word and sentence

- Make charts for the phonemes *or* and *er* with the words from the story: 'orders', 'lord', 'boring', 'for', 'story', 'further', 'casserole', 'over', 'older'. Children to list in their books.
- Groups to search for words containing the digraph '*wh*'.
- Teach that compound words are made from two words put together, with examples from the story: e.g. 'mid/night', 'foot/steps', 'no/body', 'them/selves', 'keep/sake'. Children to list.
- Teach antonyms and make a chart of examples in the story: 'top–bottom', 'highest–deepest', 'poor–rich', 'older–younger'. Children to list.
- Groups each to recite a part with expression, reflecting sense and punctuation.
- Whole story to be recited with emphasis on good performances.
- Discuss the effects of using these punctuation marks: full stops, commas, capital letters, exclamation marks, question marks and speech marks when reading out loud.

Reading

- Children to work out the meanings of unknown words: e.g. 'host', 'troupe', 'search parties', 'crockery', 'keepsake', then check in dictionary.

- Groups to decide what the story is about.
- Children to predict how the story will end:
  1. after the boy disappears;
  2. after the visit of the first daughter;
  3. before the boy goes to the underworld.
- Children to compare the setting in the castle with that in the world below.
- Groups to compare the four female characters: nurse, old widow, older daughter and younger daughter, by drawing them, writing notes and finding descriptions.

Writing

- Children to imagine a different 'other world' that a disappearing character might go to and work out a structure for a story with:
  1. beginning: how the character gets there;
  2. middle: description of setting and accounts of adventures there;
  3. end: how the character returns to the normal world.
- Children to add detail to their character studies and add ones for the lord and the boy.

Dance and drama

- Explore the idea of keeping children off the ground, and what happens when they touch it.
- Children to improvise in pairs:
  1. Nurse–boy: boy touches ground/disappears/nurse's response
  2. Old widow – boy, Older daughter – boy: boy's disappointment: other characters' joy on receiving the gold coins.
  3. Younger daughter – boy: their developing relationship.
- Groups to work on developing a play, using movement, mime and dialogue.

Art

- Drawings: the characters as part of the activities described above.
- Paintings of the other world and of the children's own other worlds.

Music

- Children to create sound effects to depict:
  1. the disappearance of the boy and the search for him.
  2. happenings at night.
  3. the other world with birds singing, animals talking, sound of gold, sound of silver and the journeying down and up.
- Children to combine these into sequences.

Y3: T2. 'The blue mountain'

Text

Many years ago there was a good king and his good queen, who lived in a fine palace on top of a hill near a river. They were happy enough but had no children. How they longed for a child!

One day a beggar woman came to the palace and told the king and queen that they would have three daughters but they must never go out of doors until they had all reached the age of fifteen. If they did a snowdrift would carry them away.

The beggar woman was fed and given money and went on her way. It was just as she promised. Before the end of that year the queen had a daughter. The next year she had another and the year after that a third daughter was born to her. Imagine how happy they were now, with three beautiful little girls!

The king and queen obeyed the warning given by the beggar woman. They kept the princesses indoors year after year. However, the day before the youngest one's fifteenth birthday, the daughters begged the guard just to let them out into the garden. The foolish man did as they asked and, immediately, a snowdrift fell and took them all away.

The king offered half the kingdom and a princess in marriage to any man who could find them. All the young nobles tried and failed. Then, one day, a captain and lieutenant in the army offered to try. So, too, did a young and very poor private. He begged the king on bended knee to let him try and the king only just let him go. He tagged along after the others.

That evening the three soldiers came to a fine mansion. It was empty so they went in. There was hardly any food in the pantry so they decided to go hunting next day. The lieutenant stayed behind to prepare the kitchen, while the captain and soldier hunted. After a while an old man on crutches came begging for a penny and, as the lieutenant handed him one, it fell on the floor. He bent to pick it up and the old man turned nasty and beat him with his crutches.

The same happened to the captain the next day, even though he had been warned by the lieutenant. On the third day it was the poor soldier's turn to stay behind. This time, when the old man asked for a penny, the soldier grabbed him by his beard and jammed it in the split in a log. Then he threatened to cut off the old man's head if he didn't tell him where the three princesses were. Terrified, and knowing he had met his match, the old man said, 'Go east to a mound and dig a square of turf from it. Lift the stone slab under the turf and let yourself down the deep hole through fire and water into the other world.'

Next day the three soldiers went east. When they reached the mound the captain went down the hole first, but the fire was too hot so he had to come back up. The lieutenant went next, but the water was too deep and cold so he too had to come back up. The poor private, though, went through the fire and water, came to the other world and found a castle. He went through many rooms then met the eldest princess, spinning copper yarn. She told him to go away because the three-headed troll would soon return. The private refused and hid. When the troll arrived they played a game with golden checkers, then the princess stroked his three heads and he fell asleep. Up jumped the private and swiped off all three heads with the troll's own sword.

Next the private went to the second princess, who was spinning silver yarn. She told him to go away because of the six-headed troll! He refused and all was as before. The troll entered, played golden checkers with the princess, had his six heads stroked, fell asleep and the soldier cut the heads off.

Then the private went to the youngest princess, who was spinning golden yarn. It was the same again, including the game with the golden checkers. This time the troll had nine heads and after they were stroked and the troll went to sleep the private swiped the lot off with the troll's massive sword.

The princesses were delighted, the youngest most of all! She tied her ring in the private's hair and they ran to the end of the tunnel. The three princesses climbed up the rope through water and fire to the top. But, as soon as they were safely on the earth, the captain cut the rope so that the private could not join them.

When they returned to the king they pretended that they had rescued the princesses. They claimed half the kingdom and two of the princesses, who were scared to tell the truth because the captain had threatened to kill them. The youngest refused to marry either of them.

The private wandered around looking for a way out, then found a tin whistle. He blew it and was surrounded by birds. One said, 'What does our master want today?' The private asked them how to get back to earth. They said only the eagle knew, so he blew it again and the big eagle came. She offered to carry the private there if he would kill twelve oxen and pop meat in her mouth during the long journey. The private did this but found it difficult to pop lumps of meat in her mouth because she was flying so fast. When they reached the king's palace she said, 'If you need me again just blow the whistle and I'll come to help you.'

Meanwhile, the princesses were unhappy. The king was concerned and asked them what was troubling them. They were afraid to tell him. The eldest pretended they were missing the golden checkers that amused them in the blue mountains. The king sent out for goldsmiths to make another set. Hearing the king's request the private, disguised as a goldsmith, offered to do the job. That night he blew the whistle and the eagle fetched the real set of golden checkers.

Next day the soldier presented the king with the checkers. He also showed the ring that the youngest princess had tied in his hair. She recognised him now and told the king what the captain and lieutenant had done. Those cruel cheats were executed for their treachery. Soon after, the private married the youngest princess and became a prince with half the kingdom. They lived happily ever after and had many children.

Word and sentence

- Make charts for the following phonemes: *ear, oo, ou, ai, ow, au, oor, ore, ea* and *u.* On them list these words, which are from the story: *ear* – 'years', 'near', 'year'; *oo* – 'good', 'took'; *ou* – 'mountains', 'cloud'; *ai* – 'mountains'; *ow* – 'how', 'however'; *au* – 'daughters'; *oor* – 'doors', 'indoors'; *ore* – 'before'; *ea* – 'beautiful'; *u* – 'beautiful'.
- In groups the children to find these words in the story and list them in their own books.

- Make a chart for words with three or more syllables. Children to find these words in the story and list them in their own books ('beginning', 'lieutenant', 'terrified').
- Using the context, children to work out definitions for these 'new' words: 'lieutenant', 'mound', 'turf', 'checkers', 'yarn', 'oxen', 'goldsmith', 'request' and 'disguise'. Check in the dictionary and add to lists.
- Compare the plural of princess (princesses) with the plural of soldier (soldiers). Children to investigate whether words ending in -s in the singular always have -es in the plural.
- Establish comma as a punctuation mark with the shortest stop between words, and that a full stop has the longest. In groups children practise reading paragraphs that show differences in the lengths of stop. Discuss.

Reading

- Draw children's attention to the following story language: 'Many years ago', 'One day', 'Then she went on her way', 'met his match', 'all was as before' and 'They lived happily ever after'. Write on a chart as examples of language used in old stories. Children to provide alternative phrases for these.
- Groups to look for and conference themes which are familiar in these stories: e.g. lowest character – poor private – becomes the hero or the use of three.
- Groups to chart good and bad characters, giving reasons based on characters' behaviour.

Writing

- Groups to identify the key incidents and record in a list, then in a storyboard.
- Children to write character portraits of a good and bad character in a letter to a friend.
- Children to write their own stories in which three characters set off in search of something valuable which is lost, following the theme of three and having encounters with characters who help them.

Dance and drama

- Explore the idea of a cloud or snowfall carrying people away to another place. Children to go beyond the ideas in the story: e.g. to another planet.
- In pairs children improvise:
  1. Daughter–soldier – she begs to be let out, he agrees, sees what happens, fears for his job.
  2. Captain or lieutenant–old man – old man asks for money, coin dropped, he beats captain/lieutenant with crutches.
  3. Private–a princess – private enters, princess tells him to go, he hides then she mimes stroking troll's head, private cuts off the heads and they run.
- Groups make a play from one part of the story, using movement, mime and dialogue and using some words from the text.

Art

- Children to draw one of the following: a princess, captain, lieutenant, king, queen, old man with the crutches, troll or the eagle. Try to get at least one illustration of each of these.
- Children to decide on their favourite scene in the story to 'illustrate' individually or in groups.

Music

- Groups to make:
  1. Sound effects to depict the disappearance of the princesses in the snowdrift.
  2. Sound effects to depict the journey down the well and into the castle.
  3. Compositions for the tin whistle.
- These to be joined and made into a composition for 'The Blue Mountain' story.

Y4: T3. 'The wonderbird'

Text

In Persia, when King Menuchir reigned, there was a great warrior called Zahon, who was wealthy and much admired, but childless. For years he prayed to the gods for a child and was eventually blessed with a son. His happiness was spoilt, though, by the fact that the boy's hair was the colour of snow and he was pitied by the other nobles because they thought the boy was from Demons and would bring bad luck.

Zahon named the baby Zal but was so distressed by Zal's colour that he took him to wild and distant mountains and left him there. The gods, however, sent Simurgh, the Wonderbird – half bird, half animal and very wise – to the little boy. It carried Zal in its claws to its nest in the cliffs. As it did so a voice said, 'Never harm the child you are carrying, Wonderbird, for he has a great future. His son will be the light of the East, the star of Persia, the Champion of the world.'

Simurgh cared for the child – even taught him to speak – until Zal was old enough to play in the mountains. Sometimes he was seen by those who passed down below and the story grew about mighty Simurgh rearing a human child.

All this time Zal's father, old Zahon, was alone, feeling guilty for abandoning his boy because his hair was white. One night he had an unforgettable dream and went to the magicians to have it interpreted. They told him it meant his son was still alive in the mountains. Zahon sent servants to where he had abandoned his son, but they found nothing.

Zahon had another dream in which a white-haired young warrior led an army on horseback. At his right hand side was a holy man who said, 'This great leader is the son you cruelly abandoned whom the gods did not forsake. His name will be great.'

This time Zahon went to the mountains himself, knelt on a rock and prayed to the gods to forgive him and bring his son back. Simurgh heard and told Zal it was time he returned to his father. Zal climbed onto the Wonderbird's wings and was carried to the rock where his father prayed. Simurgh said to Zahon, 'Here is the son you so cruelly left to die. Take care of him.'

As the Wonderbird left, Zal wept. He did not want to lose the creature who had cared for him. Simurgh blessed him and said, 'Never forget the home of your childhood and the one who looked after you. Pluck a feather from my breast and if you are ever in danger burn it and I will come and help you.' Then the Wonderbird flew to its nest and Zahon took Zal home. There he dressed him in the clothes of a prince and introduced him into the life of King Menuchir's court.

King Menuchir liked Zal and gave him a golden helmet and mace. The king's wise men predicted that Zal would be the greatest warrior. He received gifts of horses and Zahon was placed in charge of three regions of Persia. Zal prospered. His strength and fighting skills were unsurpassed. It was as if Simurgh had given him extra powers. Zal was an outstanding scholar, learning lessons from the Persian wise men.

When his father was away Zal ruled one of his regions and visited the city of Kabul. There he met Mihrab, the king of the Zohak people who were hated by the Persians. Mihrab had a daughter, Rudabeh, whose ivory-white skin, raven-black hair and cheeks of pomegranate pink impressed all who saw her. Zal longed to see her, but the palace was fortified and he knew that Menuchir would not like him to be friendly with the Zohaks. He stayed in camp.

Mihrab, however, took a liking to Zal. He told his wife and daughter about the brave and handsome governor and Rudabeh fell in love with Zal without meeting him. Her servants tried to persuade her to forget him. It was no use. Already she wanted to marry Zal. So the servants helped her by picking flowers near Zal's camp and giving a message to one of his servants, saying that Rudabeh, a princess, wanted to marry him. Zal took no persuading. He loaded horses with jewels and sent them with the servants. Rudabeh was filled with joy and wanted to meet Zal at once. But how could she without her parents knowing? Her servants suggested she tell her parents she wanted to visit a castle in the countryside then invite Zal to see her there.

Her request was granted and one evening Zal came to see her. Rudabeh, beautiful in the dying red of the sunset, smiled and talked to him from her balcony. They talked on until Zal asked for a rope so that he could climb to her. Rudabeh let down the braids of her hair and he climbed up them and into her arms. They declared their love for each other, but Zal said it must be a secret because her people were hated by his.

'I will consult my advisers before asking you to marry me,' he said. Rudabeh replied, 'My heart belongs to you. No other king can have me now.' They kissed and held each other close, then Zal lept from the balcony and was gone. At dawn the next day Zal gathered his advisers and told them of his intention to marry Rudabeh. They were worried that he wanted to marry the daughter of 'the Serpent King' and suggested he send a letter to Zahon.

Zahon asked his magicians for their advice. He was delighted when they said that the gods would bless the marriage. Furthermore, the gods foretold that a son would be born to them who would be the greatest warrior of all time. He sent this news to Zal but asked his son to keep it a secret until King Menuchir's permission was granted.

Zal and Rudabeh did not meet at this time, but sent love letters to each other. Rudabeh's mother was suspicious and asked Rudabeh what was going on. 'I am engaged to Zal. I love him more than the whole world,' she answered. Her mother was not angry but her father, Mihrab, was furious. He shouted, 'King Menuchir will take away my kingdom. He might even execute me and all this because of my daughter's selfishness!'

Mihrab's wife calmed him down and he allowed Rudabeh to come and see him. She came in her finest clothes, looking beautiful, and said at once, 'I am engaged to the noblest man in the world.' She was so happy that Mihrab hadn't the heart to tell her off. However, when King Menuchir heard of this he ordered Zahon to take an army and destroy Kabul and all its people. Mihrab found this out through his spies and knew his army would be routed. Once more his fury rose against his daughter and he even wanted to execute her. But his wife persuaded him to send Rudabeh to see Zahon, taking gifts of horses and jewels.

Zahon was impressed but would not accept the gifts for fear of King Menuchir's anger. But his love for Zal was so strong he accepted the gifts and did all he could to arrange the marriage. He went to see the king and when Menuchir heard that the magicians approved of the match he finally agreed.

All went well for Zal and Rudabeh until one day Rudabeh took ill. Her illness could not be cured. Everything the doctors tried failed. She grew weaker and weaker until she was at death's door. Zal paced the room. He tore his hair and beat his chest and shouted, 'Why didn't Simurgh leave me to die on the mountains when I was a baby?' As soon as Zal spoke the name of the Wonderbird, he remembered Simurgh's last words, 'Pluck a feather from my breast and if you are ever in danger burn it and I will come and help you.'

Zal rushed from the room and returned with the feather which he threw into the fire. Darkness came. Zal held his wife in his arms. The Wonderbird filled the room and asked, 'Why do you despair? I will cure your lovely Rudabeh and soon she will bear a son who will be called the Wonder of the World.' With those words the Simurgh gave Zal a feather from his wing and disappeared. Rudabeh sat up in bed. The pomegranate blush was in her cheeks. She smiled.

Simurgh's prohecy came true. A child was born to them called Rustem, the Wonder of the World. At the age of eight he could fight any warrior in the kingdom. He was the most handsome boy and so brave that the Persians called him their Shield but that is another story. Zal and Rudabeh grew old and their love grew stronger as they watched their son Rustem grow.

Word and sentence

- Practise chanting the names of the characters, peoples and places: Persia (per-zia), Kabul (Kar-bull), Zohak (Zoh-hack), Minuchir (Min-uh-keer), Zahon (Zar-hon), Zal (Zarl), Simurgh (Sim-erg), Mihrab (Mi-hrab), Rudabeh (Rud-ar-beh), Rustem (Rustem). Children clap the syllables and pronounce each phoneme precisely and clearly.
- Groups to:
  1. Find words with more than two syllables, list and chant them so that each syllable can be clearly heard.
  2. Work out how to say the following words and what they mean, using their knowledge of phonemes and the context: 'reigned', 'distressed', 'rearing', 'interpreted', 'unsurpassed', 'scholar', 'regions', 'braids', 'balcony', 'execute', 'despair', 'prophecy'.
  3. Find, chant and list words with -ss- in them: e.g. 'childless', 'blessed', 'distressed'. Work out meanings and check in dictionary.

4. Find words with other double letter consonants in them: e.g. 'eventually', 'suggested', and with one of the consonants in them.
5. Recite passages of about 20 lines, taking turns, responding to the punctuation marks: e.g. change to a speaking voice when there are speech marks, vary stops from full stop to comma.

Reading

- Draw children's attention to:
  1. names: e.g. Menuchir, Kabul
  2. customs: e.g. praying to the gods
  3. incidents: e.g. Zahon's visits to the mountains which suggest the story is from a different culture.
- Discuss after first reading and make a chart under the headings: Names, Customs, Incidents.
- Conference the theme of adults looking after children under these questions:
  1. Which characters are good and which are not so good parents: Zahon, Simurgh, Rudabeh's mother, Mihrab, and how is this shown?
  2. Do the not-so-good parents improve? In what ways?
  3. What are the qualities of good parenthood in the story?
  4. What do you think makes a good parent?
- Discuss the qualities of the other characters: King Menuchir, Zal and Rudabeh, encouraging the children to go beyond good/bad classifications to see all aspects of a character: although Zahon is prejudiced and cruel towards his son, he feels guilt and makes amends.

Writing

- Children to plan and write:
  1. An alternative ending to the story.
  2. The story of Rustem, basing it on prophecies about him and using chapters.
  3. A story in which different kinds of parents bring up their children now or in the future and what goes right/what goes wrong.

Dance and drama

- Explore the idea of the burning of a feather causing the appearance of a great bird, allowing the children to make their own miraculous appearances from the burning of a feather.
- Pairs to improvise:
  1. Zal–Simurgh – the Wonderbird caring for the child.
  2. Zal–Zahon – Zahon takes Zal home and prepares him for court.
  3. Mihrab–Rudabeh – she tells him she wishes to marry Zal; his response.
  4. Rudabeh's mother–Rudabeh – mother prepares her daughter for second meeting with father.
  5. Zal–Simurgh – Rudabeh is saved.

- Groups each to make a play from one part of the story, using movement, mime and dialogue and using some characters' words from the text.

Art

- Children to:
  1. Draw one of the following: Zal as a baby abandoned, Simurgh, Zahon feeling guilty, Zal dressed for Menuchir's court, Rudabeh waiting for Zal, Rudabeh 'at death's door'.
  2. Decide on their favourite scene in the story to illustrate individually or in small groups.

Music

- Groups to work out and practise compositions for the following:
  1. Zal abandoned in the wild and distant mountains.
  2. Zal at Menuchir's court.
  3. Zal and Rudabeh meeting secretly.
  4. Mihrab's reaction to Rudabeh's love for Zal.
  5. Simurgh's reappearance and curing of Rudabeh.
- Emphasise the need for variation in tempo, mood and volume in these pieces and put them together as an overture. Explain that an overture is a piece of music which contains the moods in the story and is played before the story (usually opera) is acted.

Y5: T3. 'The Steel Monster'

Text

More than a millennium ago in the great empire of Armenia there was a king with forty sons. Thirty-nine were married and it was time for the youngest one, Patikan, to seek his fortune. The king gave him a sword, a bow, a quiver full of arrows, a bag of gold and a black stallion, then wished him good luck and waved him off.

Patikan wandered the edges of the world. He saw the bright upper world and the gloomy underworld. He fought monsters and giants, wild animals and warriors and beat the lot. Eventually, his bag of gold empty, he saw a gigantic castle built of stone and steel, its turrets pushing up beyond the clouds.

Patikan rode up to the splendid fortress, followed its walls for ten miles, then stopped at the drawbridge, which was up. He looked at every window but could see no living thing. He shouted at the top of his voice, 'Whose castle is this? Does anybody live here?' There was no answer.

At dusk he heard a rumble and saw in the distance a massive figure. It was a man, or was it? He was as wide as he was high and that was very high and he was a monster. What was even more peculiar was that this monster was made of steel, except for his helmet and boots, which were copper. In his hands he held a steel bow and on his back a quiver full of copper arrows.

By now the ground shook as if an earthquake were splitting it and the Steel Monster sniffed like a hurricane. He opened his fearsome mouth and bellowed, 'I smell human flesh and I don't even have to hunt for it.' He laughed like thunder and continued:

'No birds fly over my land.
No snakes through my grass.
Nothing travels down these parts.
So you cannot pass.

Let's have a look at you. Come here or I'll set you on fire.'

Patikan drew his sword and waved it at the great thug, who shouted, 'Who do you think you are? Haven't you heard of the Steel Monster?'

'I don't *think* I'm anybody. I *know* I'm Patikan. Of course I've heard of you. I've been everywhere, killing monsters and such like, and quite fancy a scrap with you.'

The Steel Monster said, 'Phuh!' contemptuously. Patikan was blown into the nearby woods. Unperturbed, he ran back out, swung his sword and hit the Steel Monster's leg. The sword bounced back and the Steel Monster hissed fire and steam down onto him. Patikan fired arrows at the Steel Monster's head. They bounced off like matchsticks and the Steel Monster burnt them up with one little snort from his nostrils.

Nevertheless, the Steel Monster was impressed and said, 'Patikan, I admire your pluck but you have no chance. Nothing can kill me so you're wasting your time. You haven't annoyed me yet, so quit while you're still in one piece. Why not be my servant instead?' Patikan had little choice. He agreed, to save his skin. It wasn't too bad being the Steel Monster's servant. There wasn't much to do and the Steel Monster was out hunting most of the time.

The Steel Monster was in love and one day confided to Patikan, 'Everybody's afraid of me. Nothing can harm me. But I'm aching with love for the King of the East's daughter. She's gorgeous and I've already tried to abduct her seven times. Trouble is I've never been able to get hold of her without causing damage. Why don't you? If you get her for me I'll let you go free.'

Patikan agreed and set off with the Steel Monster's warnings in his ears, 'Don't try and get away. I'll kill you wherever you go.' Still, he received an amazingly fast horse and plenty of money and weapons. After a while he saw a dove with its wings trapped in a thornbush. He went over and set it free and was surprised when it said, 'One day I will repay your kindness. Take one of my wing feathers and, if ever you get into trouble, burn it and help will be yours.' The dove flew off and Patikan waved goodbye.

After three days' journeying he arrived at the city of the King of the East. He spent some of the money on the latest fashion in those parts – narrow trousers, big hat, baggy sleeved shirt – learnt how to speak the dialect and got a job in the king's gardens. One day the princess saw him through her window and liked what she saw. She leaned out and asked him over. When he saw her he trembled with excitement. She was absolutely gorgeous. 'What do you think?' she asked.

At first Patikan could not speak. But he remembered what he had come for and said, 'I wish you well. May you have a long life. I am a prince and I came here to see you. To be honest I fancy you.'

'Well,' she said, 'If that is true, you will have to pass three tests for my father and, if you fail, you will be killed. Do you still want me?'

'Yes,' he answered, 'I'm not scared, but what are the tests?'

'First you must cut down an iron pole with a wooden axe,' she said.

'What?' he answered, 'That's impossible.'

'Next you must climb a tall tree with a glass full of wine on your head without spilling a single drop,' she said.

'You must be joking!' he exclaimed.

She went on, 'Finally, a field will be planted with grains of wheat and in a day you must pick out every one even though they are mixed up with the soil.'

Patikan said, 'Your father might as well have my head now.'

She saw that he was doubtful so she said, 'Cheer up. Here's a special handkerchief. If you tie this round the iron post the wooden axe will go straight through it. And here is my precious ring. If you drop this in the wine, not a single drop will slip out when you climb the tree.'

Patikan waited, then asked, 'What about the wheat?'

'I haven't got anything special for that,' she replied.

'Ah well,' he said, 'I'll think of something when the time comes.'

Patikan joined the queue of hopefuls waiting to be tested. All the previous ones had been beheaded, but all the new ones expected to be successful. The king liked the look of Patikan. 'You know what happens if you fail, don't you?' the king asked.

'Yes, I lose my head,' Patikan answered with a smile.

Patikan was taken to the pole. He slyly tied the handkerchief to it, drew back the wooden axe and felled the pole with one stroke.

'Bravo!' exclaimed the king, pouring out a glass of wine. 'Now it's up that tree with this on your head. Remember, not a drop must be spilt.'

Patikan sneaked the ring into the wine. Up the tree he climbed and back down again without spilling the tiniest drop.

'Excellent lad!' the king shouted. 'Right. Tomorrow morning you will find the field over there planted with wheat. You must pick out every grain by sunset.'

'OK,' said Patikan glumly.

Next morning when even a few stars were still shining Patikan was picking grains. By midday his back was fit to break but he was nowhere. He sat down, stroking his neck, then remembered the dove. He took out its feather and set fire to it. As the flame died the field was a seething mass of foraging doves. They had spotted the grainsacks at the edges of the field and flew to and fro with grains so that by mid-afternoon the field was completely empty. At sunset the king's men came to inspect the field and found it grainless.

The men took Patikan to the king, who looked pleased. 'She's yours, lad. You've earned her. Stay here forever and have half of my lands if you like.'

'Thanks,' said Patikan, 'but I'd best be on my way with her.'

'As you wish,' answered the king.

Patikan and the daughter of the King of the East rode out immediately. That night when they lay side by side in the tent, Patikan placed his sword between them. The princess had noticed that Patikan was not very friendly, but this was going too far, so she asked, 'Aren't we going to be man and wife?'

'No,' he answered, 'more like brother and sister.'

She couldn't believe it. 'Then who am I marrying?' she asked.

'The Steel Monster. We're on our way to him now,' said Patikan.

'What!' she shouted, 'Him! He's been trying to abduct me for years and I've managed to escape so far. Now he's sent you to trick me and I thought you really loved me. What am I going to do?'

She was so distressed she ran to the nearby lake and was about to drown herself when Patikan shouted, 'No! Stop! Don't do it! I've got a plan.' The princess sighed with relief. The water was dark and cold. Patikan came to her and said, 'I promised I'd get you for him and there is no escaping him. But, don't worry, I'll stay with you and work out how to get you out of his clutches somehow, then marry you myself.'

'Nice idea,' she answered, 'but not much of a plan. I suppose I've not much choice though, as I love you.'

'Just like your plan with the grains of wheat, actually,' he answered smiling and then they solemnly vowed to be faithful to each other, but didn't kiss. As dawn was coming, they packed and rode to the Steel Monster's castle. The Steel Monster was delighted when he saw his servant bringing the daughter of the King of the East. He congratulated Patikan and said he could go free and take more treasure. But Patikan didn't want his freedom any more, not without the princess, so he shook his head. Strangely, the Steel Monster was a model of kindness to the princess. He said, 'You can have anything you like.'

She was smart with her answer, 'You are nice but my father made me promise that I must not sleep with my husband for seven years after the marriage. I don't break promises.'

'Now that you are mine I'm not bothered if I have to wait twenty or even forty years before we sleep together.' Then he asked Patikan if he'd like to be godfather to their first child. Patikan imagined himself as an old man being godfather to a half steel monster baby and had to stifle a laugh. He agreed, though.

So the search was now on for an idea to undo the Steel Monster and allow the lovers to be free to marry. Each had plenty but neither had one that was any good. 'Let's face it,' said Patikan, 'the Steel Monster would wake up if I tried to melt his head in the middle of the night.'

'Agreed,' laughed the princess, 'but your trick of digging a hole and covering it with branches as a trap is even worse. It would take about ten years to dig.'

When the idea did come it was like a bolt of lightning and afterwards neither of them could remember whose idea it was. This was it: Patikan would kill the Steel Monster's soul. Firstly though, the princess would have to discover where it was. For this she would have to be cunning and pretend she loved the Steel Monster.

'My love,' she said to the Steel Monster one evening after dinner, 'I miss you terribly when you go off hunting every day. I don't want to stop you going but I would love to be able to talk to your soul when you're not here. That would help me through the long day until your arrival in the evening.'

She had never shown such affection towards him before, so he believed it was because the seven years were nearly up and soon she would sleep with him. He was so besotted with her that he told her the answer straight away. 'In the white mountain seven days' ride from here lives a powerful white bull. Every seventh day he comes to drink at the marble pool. Inside the white bull there's a white fox and inside the fox a white box and inside the white box seven little white birds. My soul is in the birds. All my strength is there. Nobody can kill the white bull, but if they did the fox would escape. If the fox were caught the box would stay shut. If the box were opened the birds would fly away. So my soul and my strength are safe.'

That's what he thought. As soon as the Steel Monster was snoring, the princess ran to Patikan and told him about the white bull and the rest and added, 'Right. That's my job done. Now it's your turn. All you've got to do is kill the bull, kill the fox, get the box out of the fox, the birds out of the box and kill them too. It should be easy.'

Remembering his previous trials and no longer possessing anything like a dove's magic feather, Patikan was not so sure but was willing to give it a go. Next day he got permission from the Steel Monster to go hunting for a few days, then went to see some wise men to ask their advice. They said, 'Man is defeated by woman. The beast by wine.' That is all they said but Patikan got it. He bought seven barrels of the best red, tied them to a packhorse and rode to the white mountain.

When he got there Patikan emptied the marble pool of water and filled it with the wine. Then he jumped into a hole in the ground and waited. Fortunately, the next day was the seventh day and the white bull came ambling up for his weekly drink. This was the drink of a lifetime. One gulp and he forgot the taste was different. Two gulps and he felt like he'd never felt before. Three gulps set him mooing, four bellowing enough to cause avalanches. By the time the pool was empty the white bull was dancing over the white mountain as drunk as all the drunks that ever staggered through Armenia before and since. He collapsed.

Patikan was as quick as a butcher. He cut the bull's throat in a jiffy and in the woods the Steel Monster wailed, 'Ahhhhh! I'm a blithering idiot. Why did I tell her my secret? Patikan is slaying the white bull!' He ran home wild with rage to kill the princess.

Patikan slit open the fox before it could sniff his smell and coming out of the woods the Steel Monster was spurting blood from his nose and cursing his folly.

Patikan had the box open in a second and striding across the fields the Steel Monster saw blood shooting out of his ears and mouth. He was in a frenzy for revenge.

Patikan had the fluttering white birds as the Steel Monster approached his castle and saw the treacherous princess biting her nails in the window.

Patikan crushed two little birds. The Steel Monster's knees broke beneath him.

Patikan crushed two more little birds. The Steel Monster's arms broke and fell into the moat.

Patikan crushed two more. The Steel Monster's belly opened and out poured his guts.

Patikan crushed the last remaining bird with a rock. The Steel Monster's head shattered against the castle wall. As he collapsed thick, black smoke rose from him and drifted away like a funeral pyre.

Patikan thundered on his black stallion down from the White Mountain and into the castle courtyard. There the princess awaited him, dancing on the spot with joy. As he stopped, she leapt into the saddle beside him and said, 'Nicely done, my love. Now move forward a bit and let's get away from this place.'

They rode away into the future, were married, had lots of fun and lots of children.

Word and sentence

- Using the range of strategies that they have acquired so far, test the children's spelling of: 'millennium', 'stallion', 'eventually', 'gigantic', 'hurricane', 'fearsome', 'servant', 'gorgeous', 'remembered', 'scared', 'straight', 'precious', 'tiniest', 'jubilant', 'beastly'.
- When speaking these words emphasise pronunciation of each syllable and ask how many syllables there are.
- Pairs to use dictionaries to check each other's answers and find out the definitions.
- Children to learn those they get wrong for a re-test with the questions, 'Where was it wrong?' and 'Is there a rule?'
- Pairs to look for the following prepositions: 'up', 'in', 'on', 'at', 'into', 'onto', 'off', 'over', 'through', and to substitute other prepositions in the sentences to see what difference they make to the sense.
- Groups to recite passages of about 20 words with due attention to the punctuation by varying their performances: e.g. different voices for characters' speech, questioning tone for sentences which are questions.

Reading

- Groups to discuss themes in the story which are:
  1. similar to ones they have already read in stories: e.g. the youngest son being successful, three tasks to win the princess
  2. ones which are different: e.g. the quest for the Steel Monster's soul.
- Establish that this shows that certain themes are common in all cultures and some are particular to one or two.
- Discuss who is telling the story: Patikan? The Steel Monster?
- Establish that it is a storyteller who probably heard the story from someone else.
- Children to discuss what differences there might be if Patikan, Steel Monster or the princess told the story.
- Children to tell any part of the story in the first person from Patikan's or the princess's point of view.

Writing

- Children start to keep reading journals with pieces on:
  1. The way Patikan and the princess are with each other.
  2. What happens in their favourite part and why they like it.
  3. The discussions about similar and different themes.
  4. Predictions at various stages of the story.
  5. Any part of the story in the first person from either Patikan's or the princess's point of view.
  6. Description, explanation and commentary on the story.

Dance, drama and music

- Introduce the idea of a play which is just for voices, like you get on the radio. Say that as well as the voices of the characters there needs to be the voice of the storyteller. To make it sound realistic there also need to be sound effects and music.

● Allocate parts of the story to the groups for turning into plays for voices as described in Chapter 3, 'Scripted Plays'.

Art

● Groups to decide on favourite scenes to make into large wall paintings or banners as follows:
   1. Each child to do a drawing of a characters and background.
   2. Children then to discuss which ones they want.
   3. A smaller version of the wall painting/banner to be made as a preparation.
   4. Children to draw the main outlines using chalk or charcoal.
   5. Paint with thickly mixed, vivid colours.

Y6: T2. 'The soldier's fiddle'

Text

In a time of frequent wars, when many young men left the land for the excitement of army life, there was an ordinary soldier. Dimitry was his name. Dimitry was a happy-go-lucky sort of fellow and enjoyed the army, although he was none too keen on battle itself. He'd seen too many comrades killed in pointless wars. Good friends, too, wiped out for a little piece of land, which sometimes wasn't even worth farming. But Dimitry could put things to the back of his mind, particularly when playing the fiddle, one of his greatest joys.

Dimitry was excited. It was late afternoon on a sunny spring day and he was marching along the lanes on his way home for seven days' leave. He was awake to every little sight or sound, every sort of smell or touch. The music of the nearby stream drew him, so he put down his kit bag and soon was paddling in it, trousers rolled to the knees.

After cooling off like this, Dimitry took out his fiddle. It was a cheap thing like many country fiddlers own, but he could make it get everyone to their feet at a barn dance or send a squalling baby to sleep. Now he played a tune to remind him of home and his girlfriend, Natasha.

Behind a hazel tree somebody was hiding. A man dressed in tweeds and a deerstalker hat, a real toff. In his hand was a large net, which he swept through the air to catch butterflies. He caught one and put it in a jar and put the jar in a shiny leather bag. This man was the Devil in one of his disguises.

Dimitry was just finishing his favourite tune when the Devil approached.

'Beautiful!' he exclaimed. 'Where did you learn to play like that?'

'My dad taught me,' answered Dimitry, surprised but polite.

'Well, he did a good job.' the Devil added. 'I've not heard fiddle-playing like that before.' He paused, looking at Dimitry in a way that made the soldier feel uncomfortable. 'Let me see your violin,' the Devil asked. Without a second thought, Dimitry handed it over. The Devil plucked it and bowed it, making a dreadful racket, then gave it back.

There was a silence and Dimitry was too polite to break it. This man was obviously from a large house with acres of land and in those days a common soldier knew his place. The Devil slid a leather-bound book out of his bag. 'Look at this,' he said. 'This handsome book can make you rich beyond your wildest dreams.'

'Oh,' answered Dimitry. Something wasn't right but he didn't know what it was. This man was too familiar as if he was his long lost uncle or something. Dimitry opened the book and saw figures and astrological signs. He was not much of a reader and, after glancing at a few pages, he handed it back, saying, 'Sorry, but I don't read very well.'

The Devil sat down next to him, opened the book and explained its powers. 'These signs and symbols,' he said, 'can tell the future, particularly valuable for making forecasts involving the acquisition of money.'

'Acquisition of money?' asked Dimitry, 'What do you mean?'

'Acquisition of money, yes, getting money by making bets or investments, that sort of thing is what the book can do. You could work out the winner of a horse race or, better still, what stocks and shares are going to go through the roof during the next few days.'

Dimitry couldn't believe his ears. 'No,' he said, 'That's not possible.'

'Oh yes,' replied the Devil, 'I'm serious. Look, I'll make a bargain with you. You give me your fiddle and come to my house for three days to teach me how to play it. In return I will give you this book and teach you how to use it to your own advantage. What do you say?'

Dimitry was tempted. His wages were small and he spent most of it on Natasha. If he came into a bit of money, he could ask Natasha to marry him straight away without having to wait till he had scraped together enough to get a room somewhere.

'No, I couldn't.' Dimitry replied. The Devil knew he was tempted.

'Just think of what you could do with a bit of money in the bank,' he said, wheedlingly. 'You could buy your own house and fill it with furniture for your lady love. You could have children and send them off to school. Why be hard up all your life, scrimping and saving to rent a room? What sort of life is that for a young couple?'

It was easy. After a few minutes, Dimitry handed over his fiddle, took the book and stepped into the Devil's walnut coach with its four black stallions. The Devil jumped into the rider's seat, shook the reins and the horse went off at break-kneck speed. Dimitry felt the coach lift and saw trees whizz past his face. Within minutes they were slowing down along a straight drive towards a mansion in a splendid estate.

Three days of absolute luxury! Imagine anything you would like to eat or drink, anything – at the click of the Devil's fingers. Dimitry spent the whole time with his eyes wide open. He was never bored, not for one moment. The lessons didn't take too long, either. Dimitry taught the Devil a few tunes, which he played quite well, and the Devil taught him how and when to use the book to best advantage.

All 'good' things come to an end and, after three days had passed, Dimitry was back again on a late sunny spring afternoon marching down past the stream where he first met the Devil.

'OK, so I've lost my fiddle, but I've got the book. If I want I could buy a Stradivarius – the best fiddle money can buy – with what I'll make. Nothing bad has happened, except I've lost three days of leave. Lost! I've had a great time. I'll soon make it up to Natasha and when she finds out that we'll be rich, well she'll change her tune that's for sure . . .'

Dimitry gibbered on like this until he came to the familiar rise above his home village.

He looked down as day darkened. Lights ripened like waxed apples in windows. Blue curls of wood smoke drifted from chimneys and the last tunes of children's games rang out. The village was getting snug for the night. Dimitry heard a call – old Yuri shouting at his stubborn goat. He called out to his old friend, 'Yuri, is that you? It's Dimitry over here. Can't you see me? Yuri!' Yuri was snatching at the rope tied to his Billy goat. He looked up, startled. When he saw Dimitry his eyes opened wide and his mouth even wider. He dropped the rope and ran off down the hill. Dimitry looked at himself to see if something was different, but he was just as he had been all the way home. A little dusty, perhaps, but that shouldn't bother Yuri. He was a scruffy old farmer who wore the same clothes all the time.

Puzzled, Dimitry walked slowly down to the village. Next, he saw Anya, who kept chickens in the old barn. She was feeding them and clucking at the huge flock around her. When she saw Dimitry the bowl flew out of her arms. She stumbled over her chickens and in through the back door of her cottage, white-faced and horrified.

Dimitry began to panic. These were people he had known all his life, people who had always liked him. To check things out, he went into The Woolpack Inn, already quite full with farmhands having a quick drink on the way home from work. He knew every one of them. They were his mates. He called out, 'Hello there, I'm home on leave. See you all later for a drink.' In reply they turned away, grasping their pint mugs, muttering. He heard 'deserter' whispered by one and 'escaped from prison' from another.

Dimitry left the pub, shaking with terror and running down the main street to his house. When he got there, he didn't knock. He sneaked into the garden and peeped in through the back window. His mum was there, looking a little older. His dad was there, hobbling round on a stick. He'd never seen that before. Suddenly, his mum saw his face at the window. She shrieked and hurried out of the room.

Dimitry's world was changed. For a final check, he walked across to Natasha's parents' house and peeped through the little round window in the front door. Natasha, looking older and plumper, was changing a baby's nappy. A toddler was pulling at her apron saying, 'Mummy come and look, come and look.' Opposite in an armchair sat a man, reading the paper. A happy family scene with Natasha, his girlfriend, at the centre. But now she was another man's wife!

He trudged through the main street past windows with drawn curtains. Even the familiar old sheep dog barked and growled at him as he left the village and climbed back up the hill.

'Three days,' he said. 'Three days! What's going on?'

As he mused like this, leaning against a tree, a gypsy-looking man came up to him. The face was familiar. 'What's the matter?' he enquired. 'Why do you look so glum?'

It was that toff's voice, but not quite. There was a slight accent in it now, as if he was from somewhere near Moscow. He asked again, 'What's the matter with you? Have you lost something . . . ?'

'I've lost myself,' answered Dimitry, and at once he knew who he was talking to. All his spirit drained out of him as if disappearing into the ground.

The Devil became domineering. 'Pull yourself together, lad,' he commanded. 'It was a bargain, right? You have the book. Use it! Change your life. Forget that petty crew down there. They're not worth a second thought. Just a bunch of peasants without ambition. You have the book. You can go far. Now use it!' Then the Devil left.

Dimitry marched through the night. He marched into dawn, knowing in his heart that three days was three years when you took a break with the Devil.

Dimitry was sitting in an inn, drinking his morning tea, when he heard a group of farmers, in town for market day, talking about a horse race that afternoon. They had newspapers laid out on the table and were discussing the form of each horse. He followed them to the racing track and consulted the book. He still had a week's wages and placed it all on a four-way bet. Having no real interest in horse racing, he went into a field, lay down and fell into a deep and troubled sleep. When he woke, he was shaking, then he remembered where he was and went to the bookie.

All Dimitry's horses had won. He had increased his money by about twenty times. He wasn't yet rich, but he was on his way. The strange thing was that he didn't feel much happier. He went back into the town, booked in at a hotel and bought some clothes. He had a bath, put on his new clothes and dined in the hotel.

Dimitry stayed in that town throughout race week and, by the end of it, all the bookies refused to take any more of his bets. There was nothing left for him there, so he left for the city in his own horse and carriage.

The city was a frightening place to Dimitry, but he had plenty of money so he quickly settled down, waited on hand and foot wherever he went. After a few days, he found the stock exchange, where men buy stocks and shares in companies. If a company succeeds, the value of your shares goes up. If a company fails, they go down. Dimitry studied the book every night and it told him where to invest his money.

By the end of the first week he was a millionaire. By the end of the first month he was a multi-millionaire. By the end of the year he was living in his own mansion on the outskirts of the city, employing hundreds of people to do jobs for him and spending most of his days potting reds in his oak panelled snooker-room or sailing his yacht out at sea.

Dimitry had plenty of girlfriends now. None of them would have cared if he had been missing for three years instead of three days. None of them felt anything at all for him, really. It was his money and lifestyle they liked. He also had plenty of business associates, but they didn't care either. In the world of the multi-millionaire nobody cares much about anything, except making more money which they no longer need.

Dimitry was bored. He had not become happy. The last time he was happy was when he played his fiddle down by the stream. One evening, when he was potting a black, he remembered the old days and the tears flowed down his cheeks. He began to curse his bad luck out loud. His servant came over and asked was there anything wrong and all Dimitry could say was, 'Yes, everything.' The servant thought how ungrateful the rich are and left him.

Soon, however, he was back, this time accompanied by an old lady selling things from a basket. The servant explained that he had done everything he could to get rid of her, but she refused and was so strong he couldn't throw her out.

'It's all right,' said Dimitry. 'I don't mind talking to an old pedlar lady. It might relieve the boredom for a while.'

'Still not satisfied?' asked the pedlar lady, and Dimitry knew who she was. 'Would you like to buy something from me, kind sir?' she asked.

Dimitry looked into the basket and saw, among the ribbons and other trifles, his old fiddle. 'Would you like to buy this fiddle?' asked the pedlar lady.

'Yes, I would,' answered Dimitry and stuffed notes into her hand. He took up the fiddle, put it under his chin, took up the bow and drew it across the strings. The sound that came out was diabolical, a noise to waken the dead. Dimitry had lost everything he cared about. He threw the fiddle away and cursed the Devil.

'Look what you have,' said the Devil. 'What more could you want?'

'To be an ordinary man with a wife and kids in an ordinary village, working for my wages and seeing my mates in the pub on a Saturday night. That's all I want and that is what I can't have.'

The Devil threw the notes back at him, took the violin and left, laughing.

That night, when all were asleep, even the moon and stars, Dimitry took the book, tore the pages out and burnt them by the side of the swimming pool. The ashes were fluttering into the water as he picked up his bag and left the mansion. Dimitry marched again. He looked like a soldier home on leave, except that his face was lined with despair. He marched through the night. The clouds left the moon and stars alone and the road before him was turned into a silver trail. Soon after midnight, he passed through a wood and reached the frontier between his and another country. The border guards were nowhere to be seen, and he'd had enough of life in his own country, so he crossed into the new land without hesitation.

As he marched further into the new terrain, his spirits lifted and he felt the slightest shade of happiness for the first time since meeting the Devil. As dawn came, he saw another town. Shadows of clouds raced across it, tinged with the red of sunrise. It was a town of thin steeples and elegant turrets. Time for a second fresh start, but this time without the wretched book that had turned him greedy.

Later, Dimitry was sitting outside another inn, eating breakfast in the sun among hanging flower baskets. He watched the people going about their business, speaking a language he could understand. He felt relaxed. He felt free, until a cattle farmer sat opposite him. This man wore a large, floppy hat which cast a shadow over his face, so that Dimitry could not see his features very well. He spoke with a drone in a broad country accent.

'You're not from these parts, are you?' he asked. 'What brings you here. Business?' There was an over-familiar tone to his voice. 'Travelled far, have you, and by the look of you, on foot?' Dimitry tried to ignore him, averting his face to look at a horse, but it was difficult. The cattle farmer was insistent with his questions. 'You haven't crossed the frontier, have you, without a passport?' Dimitry was saved from answering these difficult questions by a loud noise. It was a brass band playing the sort of tune normally kept for funerals. The band was leading a procession but, although the people were serious, nobody wore black and nobody cried.

The procession stopped, and a man in a splendid red uniform, braided with gold, stepped onto a box, placed before him by a boy. He pulled out a scroll, cleared his throat and bellowed, 'Hear ye, hear ye! His majesty wishes to inform you that his daughter, her royal highness the princess Penelope, is so sick she is almost dying. She will neither eat nor drink and doctors from all parts of the kingdom have failed to cure her. His majesty is, therefore, offering a reward to any man who can find that cure: half of the kingdom and the princess Penelope's hand in marriage.'

The man rolled up the scroll, put it away, stood down, signalled to the band, the box was taken away and the procession went to another part of the town. The cattle farmer took off his hat, leaned on the table with both of his elbows, stared Dimitry straight in the eye and said, 'Go on, lad. Here's your chance. Why not have a go? Nothing ventured, nothing gained. Give it a whirl. Have a go. What have you to lose?'

Dimitry knew who it was who had come to blight him again. He returned the Devil's direct look, and replied, 'You rotten cheat, you! Why can't you leave me alone? What is it you want from me? You've already ruined my life!'

Instead of answering Dimitry's questions, the Devil merely continued his own theme. 'You say your life is ruined. OK. So what are you going to do about it? Mm? Spend your days whinging into your beer? Turning into a loser? A has-been? A nobody? Go on then, go on. But here's your main chance. Go and cure the king's lovely daughter, Penelope, and settle down as a prince. Not bad for peasant boy who went a-soldiering, hey?'

Dimitry knew the Devil had won again. Yes, this was a challenge indeed. He might find love, companionship, honour . . . who knows? He drank his coffee to the grains but, when he looked up to reply, there was nobody there. However, despite this reminder of everything that had gone wrong, Dimitry went to the royal palace. He approached the gates, said what his business was and was shown into a room. Nobody else was there and he was kept waiting a long time.

Dimitry found a pack of cards left on a table. He sat down, took out the cards and dealt himself a hand of poker. Five cards, and all of them hearts! A flush. Ten-Jack-Queen-King-Ace of hearts. He shuffled the pack and dealt himself another hand. It was exactly the same. He looked up, and there was the Devil again, this time wearing a butler's uniform. Yes, he was smartly dressed in black with a red waistcoat, and was smoking a large cigar.

'Care for a hand?' he asked.

Dimitry remembered something he had heard as a child. 'The Devil only has power over those in debt to him.' Dimitry didn't have the book but he still had a roll of bank notes gained from the book. If he could lose it all to the Devil, he might escape his power.

'Gladly,' answered Dimitry, 'would you like me to deal?'

'Of course,' answered the Devil.

They played, and every hand Dimitry got, whether dealt by himself or by the Devil, was a losing hand. But Dimitry bet heavily on all of his hands as if they were the very best. The Devil was winning all Dimitry's bank notes and didn't know how to stop. For once, Dimitry was outwitting him. It was as if, by remembering those simple childhood days, he had released himself from the Devil's grasp.

'Raise you ten thousand,' said Dimitry, laying his last notes on the table.

'I'll see you,' exclaimed the Devil in a panic.

Dimitry laid his cards on the table. Two of clubs. Five of diamonds. Three of spades. Ten of spades. Four of hearts. A useless hand.

In a high voice the Devil squeaked, 'Ten high! All you have is ten high! What are you playing at? I have three aces and two kings, a hand worth betting on. Why are you so reckless with your money?'

'It's no longer my money,' answered Dimitry, 'it's all yours!' He noticed his fiddle leaning against the Devil's chair, snatched it up and started to play it. The music was beautiful and resonated around the room as if Dimitry were a concert violinist.

The Devil writhed and choked. He grabbed his throat. His eyes buckled like broken bicycle wheels as he flew, shouting, through the open window, 'Don't think you have won the war just because you've won this battle. I'll be back, wait and see!'

Dimitry laughed at this amazing performance, as a servant entered the room, saying, 'Would you like to come this way?' Dimitry followed up the red-carpeted stairs and into the princess Penelope's bedroom. There was an atmosphere of deep solemnity in the place as if everybody expected Penelope to die. She was lying on a four poster bed, hung with netting.

Dimitry shuddered, but then strode forward, chalked his bow, placed his fiddle under his chin and played the most beautiful tune he could remember. It was one his father taught him when he had the fiddle for his tenth birthday. As he played, the servants in the room began to weep. As he played, it seemed that light was illuminating dark corners of the room. As he played, the princess stirred. Her eyelids opened to reveal the blue buds of her eyes and, glistening in each, was a tear like fresh morning dew.

Penelope sat up in her bed for the first time in six months saying, 'I'm starving! Why is there no food? It's well past breakfast time.'

Dimitry pulled the netting from the bed and played another tune, a merry jig. The princess smiled, jumped out of bed and danced. Meanwhile, in the gardens, the Devil – now a poisonous snake – slithered down a hole in the ground. Penelope danced around the room to Dimitry's wild tunes and the king and queen entered. Dimitry stopped but the king waved a hand at him and said, 'Carry on. Please, please, carry on. This is the most wonderful sight in the world!'

Later Penelope and Dimitry ate a hearty lunch in the grand hall. They chatted and giggled as if they had known each other for years. The king and queen watched them from the other end of the table. They were speechless as they saw the flush return to their daughter's cheeks and she smiled with newly-awakened love.

The courtship of Dimitry and Penelope did not last long. They were engaged that afternoon and married three days later in the biggest event the kingdom could remember. Partying lasted a month and very little work was done in any of the four corners of the kingdom.

Now reader, you may think I have reached that moment when something like 'lived happily ever after' will conclude the story of the soldier and his fiddle, but I haven't. There are two possible endings. One is tragic and one is nearly tragic. The tragic one is told first, the nearly tragic one second, but you will need to decide which of them is true. I have to say that the tragic ending to this story is the old one and the nearly tragic one is the new. If you don't like either of them, you will have to make up one of your own.

Here is the tragic ending of 'The Soldier's Fiddle':

One spring morning, years later, when they were chatting about the day ahead, Penelope asked questions she had never asked before. 'Where do you come from, my love? Where do your mother and father live? Have you any brothers and sisters?' The questions tumbled from her tongue. 'Let us visit your parents and bring them here to live out their last years in comfort.'

Dimitry had thought about these things already, but rejected them. He knew that his happiness only returned when he came into this kingdom. He knew he wouldn't have a second chance if he threw this one away and remembered the last words of the Devil, 'Don't think you have won the war just because you've won this battle.'

So he tried to put her off with all sorts of lame excuses. 'I haven't seen them for years. They'll have forgotten me. They won't want to see me.' He knew, as he said them, that she would sweep them aside. By the time she did, Dimitry had given in. One look from her and he could refuse nothing.

They took a coach and drove to the frontier where one of the horses broke loose and bolted, leaving the coach in a ditch. Dimitry went to get the horse, leaving Penelope by the wayside. As he crossed the frontier, out leapt the Devil, cackling and dancing. He led Dimitry away, head bowed like a prisoner. The Devil had won and the moral of the story is, 'Don't try to add to what you have, what you once had.' Penelope was left lamenting the loss of her only love and father to her children.

A bleak ending with a moral. Fine, if that's how you like your stories to end. But what about the new one? Where does the course of that fateful morning end? Does Dimitry persuade Penelope to give up her hopeless longings? No. Does the weather turn stormy? No. Are all the horses struck down with a terrible disease? No. Do the wheels fall off the carriage as it leaves the palace? No.

This is what happened:

As the carriage neared the frontier, Dimitry turned stiff with fear. His face went white. His eyes opened wide with horror and he gripped the seat tightly. He said nothing, for words could not get out of the thin slit that his mouth had become. Penelope noticed this and shouted to the coach driver to stop. She opened the door of the coach and asked Dimitry to come to the side of the road with her. She didn't ask him what was wrong. She knew. She had never known Dimitry to behave like this before. To her, he was a loving husband, a father full of fun and games. A happy man, whatever he did. Now he was a nervous wreck, just because of a whim she had.

'My love,' she said, standing before him, 'I no longer wish to go to your old country and I know you don't.'

'No . . . no . . .' he stammered, trying to think of something to say.

'Don't speak,' she replied. 'I am going to have my own way. Coachman, turn the coach around and take us home.' They got back on the coach and, as the horses broke into a trot, the Devil slid from behind a tree, spat poison aimlessly into the air and wriggled down the hole in the ground, where he had come from.

Word and sentence

- Using the range of strategies that they have acquired so far, children to learn and be tested on the following lists of words for spelling:
    1. 'frequent', 'comrades', 'beloved', 'fractious', 'butterflies', 'disguises', 'astrological', 'acquisition', 'magnificent', 'luxury'.
    2. 'exchange', 'enormously', 'millionaire', 'associates', 'accompanied', 'diabolical', 'ruined', 'ordinary', 'frontier', 'hesitation'.

3. 'resonated', 'atmosphere', 'solemnity', 'proclaimed', 'poisonous', 'slithered', 'tragic', 'traditional', 'excuses', 'loose', 'lamenting', 'nervous', 'wreck', 'wriggled'.

- When you speak these words emphasise pronunciation of each syllable and ask how many syllables there are.
- Pairs use dictionaries to check each other's answers and find out the definitions.
- Children to learn and be retested on wrong ones with the questions: 'Where was it wrong?' and 'Is there a rule?'
- Revise 'active' and 'passive' voice:
  1. Active voice – sentence/phrase in which the subject is the person/thing acting upon something (e.g. line 12 '. . . he was marching along the byways . . .').
  2. Passive voice – sentence/phrase in which the subject is the person/thing acted upon by the verb (e.g. lines 5–6 'He'd seen too many comrades killed . . .').
- Pairs read at least 30 lines, underlining active verbs in red and passive verbs in blue.
- Discuss the results as a class, asking the children to decide who is the more active, Dimitry or the Devil, and is there any way of proving this?

Reading

- In groups children to investigate these aspects of narrative structure:
  1. What phrases does the writer use to indicate time or the passing of time? e.g. 'It was late afternoon . . .' and '. . . after three days had passed . . .'.
  2. How does the writer indicate a change in the plot? e.g. 'Dimitry began marching through the night.' i.e. there is a journey involved.
  3. How successful is the writer in presenting the Devil in his various disguises? Children to compare the different ways the Devil is introduced. Does the reader know immediately that it is the Devil? Or is there a feeling of mystery at first? Discuss.

Writing

- Discuss the two different endings to the story. Which one do the children prefer? Which is more realistic? Children to write their own endings to the story.
- Tell the children that 'The Soldier's Fiddle' is one a several stories in which a character 'sells his soul to the Devil'. And that the soul can be represented as something precious to the owner of it. Children to plan and write their own stories on this theme.
- Ask the children to be aware of ways of indicating time and its passage, change in the plot and ways of introducing the Devil.
- Children to write plot summaries, character studies and reviews of the story for children in other classes to read.

Dance and drama

- Using the plot of the story, children to improvise a whole-class play.
- When the children have produced a play that works, they should write it into a script then compare it with the original story. Do they wish to make any changes to the script? For instance, is the language interesting or powerful enough?
- Perform the final play to the school, perhaps with an invited audience.

Art

- Groups to make large wall hangings to be used for each scene in the play. These could either be of locations: e.g. Penelope's bedroom; or more abstract: e.g. coloured patterns to represent Dimitry's feelings of despair.

Music

- Children to compose musical interludes to indicate the changes in the plot or to introduce each new scene.

References

1. Goody, J. (1992) 'Oral culture' in Bauman, R. (ed.) *Folklore, Cultural Performances and Popular Entertainments*, 12. London: Oxford University Press.
2. Goody (1992) 12.
3. David, A. and M. E. (eds). (1964) 'Introduction', *The Frog King and Other Tales of the Brothers Grimm*. New York: Signet Classics.
4. Zipes, J. (1983) *Fairy Tales and the Art of Subversion*, 10. London: William Heinemann.
5. Carter, D. (1987) *The Odyssey Project*. Mold: Clwyd Education Authority.
6. Propp, V. (1982) *Theory and History of Folklore*. Manchester: Manchester University Press.
7. Bettelheim. (1976) *The Uses of Enchantment*. Harmondsworth: Penguin Books.
8. Bettelheim (1976) 7.
9. Zipes (1983) 12.
10. Bettelheim (1978) 8.
11. Bettelheim (1978) 37.
12. Bettelheim (1978) 37.
13. Bettelheim (1978) 37.

Chapter Five

The classical inheritance

What is a 'classic'?

The word 'classic', like many words, has passed from a particular to a general use. It is a word which can be appended to anything, even the brand name of a cigarette, the 'Marlborough Classic'. It is in the nature of certain words in any language to assume a sort of chameleon relationship with meaning. 'Classic' is one of these. Consequently, 'classic' is used as often as ever and right across the social spectrum. It has both a mainstream use and, among the young, a subcultural use. In millennium Britain, therefore, it is possible to hear, 'Do you like my Levi 501's? Classic!' or 'Beckham beat two men and let go a pinpoint cross. Yorke stole in on the blind side and headed into the top corner. A classic goal!'

The word 'classic' has acquired two main and interconnected shades of meaning. These are to do with 'high quality' on the one hand and 'tradition' on the other. In the examples above it is not only that the jeans and the goal are high in quality. There is the sense that these phenomena have pedigrees going back years. The jeans have not only been available for a long time in their own right but fit in with a tradition of comfortable, hard-wearing and stylish trouserwear. The goal, also, has two traditional elements to it. It is brought about by the tradition of defeating a defence by 'going wide' or 'down the wing' and crossing the ball accurately. Thus, David Beckham does something Stanley Matthews used to do. The other tradition is that of the striker deceiving the defence by sneaking in behind them and deflecting the cross away from the goalkeeper and Yorke is the equivalent of Stan Mortensen. So, high quality is somehow made higher by the adherence to tradition. The traditional shade of meaning is important as a sort of stamp or seal of approval. It aids us when making judgments. The evaluation of something entirely new presents us with problems. In a sense, we have to create our own set of judgment criteria, unless we are happy to say something is 'good' simply because we like it.

The word 'classic', though, refers back to something most people have little or no experience of, the arts of Ancient Greece and Rome. The reason for the importance of the term 'classic' is connected with the fact that those arts revolutionised the development of the vernacular cultures of Europe in the fifteenth and sixteenth centuries. It was their discovery that caused the Renaissance, which affected art, literature, music, drama, dance and architecture for many centuries to come. The word 'classic' also identified a whole system of education for the aspiring middle classes. So, to use the Encarta encyclopaedia definitions, although 'classic' is used 'primarily to denote and characterize a type and style or period of creative work' which means 'any ancient Greek or Roman literary work of the highest quality', it more often means, 'any work accepted either as a model of excellence or as a creation of enduring cultural relevance and value'.[1]

This definition, with its 'model of excellence' and 'enduring cultural relevance', offers a valuable criterion or benchmark for making judgments about works for use in primary classrooms. It is a criterion already in use as seen in the article 'On the permanence of Pooh' by Chris Powling. Although acknowledging that certain things are outdated in the Pooh books, Powling has no doubts about their enduring appeal. They have a 'luminious what-did-I-tell-you quality, a celebration of the obvious . . . verbal deftness . . . success at storytelling'. Most of all, however, 'The world Pooh creates is completely unique and utterly self-sustaining. Yes, it is a world that's very like ours . . . but much, much more like itself.'[2]

In this article Powling is identifying both the quality of writing in the Pooh stories and the enduring relevance of its 'world'. That world is relevant because it is like our own and true to itself. Now these criteria apply in equal measure to fiction in general and to fiction written specifically for children and this raises a further question. Are there any essential differences? Neither the fairy tales and folk tales nor the myths and legends were made especially for children. Indeed, apart from schoolbooks, no books were published for children until the 1740s, a mere 250 years ago. Until then children who could read made use of the books available to adults. For many years after that there were no works of fiction especially written for children.

In this respect it is worth looking at the childhood reading matter of writers who rose to prominence in the nineteenth century. For instance, one of the novelist George Eliot's most treasured early books was a bird book called *A Linnet's Life*. She said of this book: 'It made me very happy when I held it in my little hands and read it over and over again; and thought the pictures beautiful, especially the one where the linnet is feeding her young.'[3]

John Clare, from a poor background, began with '6py Pamphlets that are in the possession of every door calling hawker and found on every bookstall at fairs and markets'.[4] Such pamphlets were available to all and consisted mainly of folk tales and ballads. But there was no fiction written especially for children in either writer's experience.

Before children's fiction became a genre in its own right, the most popular work for children was Jonathan Swift's *Gulliver's Travels*. An interesting account of the appeal of this book is found in Charlotte Bronte's description of Jane Eyre's reading habits as a child. Jane has only a passing interest in Bewick's *History of British Birds*, she dips into Richardson's *Pamela* and tries to read history books, but her joy is in Swift's fiction: 'This book I had again and again perused with delight. I considered it a narrative of facts, and discovered in it a vein of interest deeper than what I found in fairy tales . . .'[5]

Jane Eyre, age ten, goes on to remark on the fading delights of fairy tales, having tried in vain to find elves and fairies in flowers and under leaves. However, she actually believes in Lilliput and Brobdingnag as 'solid parts of the earth's surface' which 'one day, by taking a long voyage' she might 'see with (her) own eyes'.[6]

Here, in a 'vein of interest deeper than what I found in fairy tales', we have a variation of Powling's idea of 'permanence'. Lilliput and Brobdingnag are worlds 'very like ours . . . but much, much more like [themselves']. On the one hand they depend for their existence on truths about people and circumstances in the real world. On the other they are integrated by their own particular characters and structures. Lilliput, for instance, while revealing truths about the pettiness of the leaders of eighteenth century England, is posited on the fact that the people are 'not six inches high'. In *Gulliver's Travels* Swift is particularly strong in creating other worlds which are 'very like ours' yet 'much more like themselves' and much of this is achieved through his style. He set out to write the satire in the style of a travel book, which anybody who could read would understand and accept as 'real'. The prose is a perfect example of factual writing, yet contains the most unbelievable 'facts'. This, at once makes the satire sharper and the whole work more readable. Certainly, Jane Eyre finds it so readable she reads it 'again and again' and believes in its truth emphatically.[7]

That *Gulliver's Travels* is a 'classic' work of fiction, nobody would dispute. It is also a 'classic' work of fiction for children. It can stand up to scrutiny by any definitions of the word 'classic' other than being a work from Ancient Greece or Rome. Even on this count it passes to a certain extent, being a product of eighteenth century neo-classicism. In a sense, however, being a 'classic' is insufficient. Teachers must ask the question, 'why should a work such as this be taught in a school?'

Why teach classic works of literature in the primary school?

Another word frequently used as an alternative to 'classic' is 'great'. Thus the works of Shakespeare are 'great' and Shakespeare himself is 'great'. If a work is 'great', one argument goes, 'it should be taught to children in school'. This was an important criterion for the Cox committee when constructing the National Curriculum orders for English and is a spurious argument for justifying works for inclusion in the curriculum.[8] Education is not part of the heritage industry. A 'great works' curriculum for English would most likely switch children off because it would be accompanied by a 'great works' mentality in the educational use of the texts. This 'great works' mentality would look at a work like *Gulliver's Travels* as a great landmark of the eighteenth century enlightenment, which should be taught to children. In other words, the emphasis would be on the wrong side of the equation, on the greatness of the work rather than on the educational requirements of children.

A work of literature, though 'great' in itself, may not be 'great' in the primary classroom. It will only be great as a text for children if it concurs with their interests, psychological needs and potential for understanding. However, it would be equally misconceived to serve children material which concurs with these three things but which is not high in quality and is, therefore, insufficiently challenging. Any work of literature will be great along the lines argued here, if it provides for children's developmental needs at the same time as providing cultural challenge. A work will be great insofar as it has levels of challenge beyond the story, offering access to the understanding of the human condition which might or might not be a little out of reach.

The addiction to soap operas, which most children have acquired over the last ten years or more, can be viewed in two ways. The great works as heritage attitude is that soap operas 'dumb down' the taste of the people. We have all heard this argument and many of us who are parents and teachers have joined in with it. We fear that our children's sensibilities will be adversely affected by watching Neighbours every night and Eastenders two or three times times a week. When we hear the prattle on Saturday morning television, our children lying around in their pyjamas with a bowl of breakfast cereal in their hands, we fear that they are losing something we have got. The facts are often very different from this. We need to ask ourselves why our children can so easily be 'hooked' on the plights of older teenagers and adults in fictions which involve issues traditionally considered well beyond the domain of childhood. Surely we must have it wrong for, often, some of those same children are seen with their heads tucked into Tolkien's *Lord of the Rings* or gripped by a video of Jane Austen's *Sense and Sensibility*.

Adults have consistently patronised their children's tastes in fiction for hundreds of years and most of us are guilty of it. Many parents think that the fictions which their children experience should have U certificates. If, however, *Gulliver's Travels* were assessed for suitability on grounds, for instance, of indecency, many passages in Book 2 (Brobdingnag), Book 3 (The academy at Lagado) and Book 4 (The sexual behaviour of the Yahoos) would acquire 18 certificates. Even Book 1 (Lilliput) would move out of the U, PG and 12 categories when Gulliver extinguishes a fire by urinating on it!

A crucial interest and need of childhood is to know about adulthood. When Margaret, age eleven, in *Sense and Sensibility*, is asked to go for something when her sister Marianne is injured, her demand of 'Don't say anything important while I'm away'[9] is a cry from the heart that most children would appreciate. So, part of growing up is coming to terms with the idea of being grown up. This does not mean that children should 'lose' their 'childhoods' or grow old before their time. It means that they should be allowed to encounter aspects of the full human condition, not merely of the condition of childhood. Encountering these things in fiction is a safe way of doing this. In fiction children are protected from the consequences of a wide variety of actions but can experience the actions themselves, the reasons for the actions and the consequences. This vicarious contact with experience is one of the purposes of fiction.

The implication of these arguments is that we need to broaden our definition away from 'children's fiction' and into one of 'fiction for children'. We need to say that fiction written specifically for children is not enough, providing an insufficient experience of the world past, present and future and failing to reach the full heights of excellence which our children deserve. To summarise, while they obviously need to engage with the full range of fiction written specially for them, children need and deserve access to 'great' works which have become pillars of the culture, not only Roald Dahl but also Charles Dickens, not only *Tom's Midnight Garden* but also *The Tempest*.

Literacy strategy lessons

The Literacy Strategy lessons in this chapter present texts which have been chosen in an attempt to meet these requirements. For each age group a text has been chosen which, in the opinion and experience of the author, meets the requirement of excellence and of traditional acceptance. There is nothing particularly unusual or radical in the choice. From the prince who wants a real princess through to the prince who is shipwrecked in a storm, the full primary age range is covered.

Every work of classical fiction should be introduced in the following way:

- Make large poster versions of the two extracts.
- Read the story, in episodes from Year 2 on, to the children, inviting Reception and Year 1 children to join in with repetitions.
- Establish that they remember each episode by going over the main points.
- Pairs or groups to retell the story to each other with the listeners making corrections.
- Briefly recap the story at the start of each session.
- Groups to recite extracts of the text, rehearsing briefly every day. Give advice on pronouncing each sound correctly.
- Teach children how to change their voices for different characters and for punctuation marks and emphasis. Allow time for experimentation with this.
- When the groups have reached a good level of clarity and expression in speaking their passages they should perform to the whole class.
- Word and sentence level work is based on the two extracts of text provided in each set of notes. However, you might like to use other extracts in addition.
- Work based on every story should conclude with the following kinds of plenary or sharing:
  - Frequent revision of word work items with regular chanting of the sounds.
  - Children to practise retelling the story in their own words and reading parts of it, paying due attention to punctuation.
  - Plays and dances to be rehearsed and performed to audiences, sometimes invited from other classes. Musical pieces to be performed as part of these occasions.
  - Art to be exhibited in classroom or corridor galleries.
  - Writing to be anthologised and put on display.

YR: T3. Hans Andersen, 'The Princess and the Pea'[10]

Although Andersen drew on the folk tradition for his tales, his approach was different from that, say, of the Brothers Grimm, who attempted to convey the stories they collected as faithful to the original version as was possible. Andersen developed his own style, writing the stories '. . . just the way I would tell them to a child.'[11] Andersen was also different because he derived many of his stories from literary rather than oral stories. His voice in the stories is also different, being very much his own. His tales are literary, his style individual. Here is the complete text of 'The Princess and the Pea'.

Text

There was once a prince. He wanted a princess, but it had to be a true princess! So he journeyed all around the world to find one, but no matter where he went, something was wrong. There were plenty of princesses, but whether or not they were true princesses he couldn't find out. There was always something that wasn't quite right. So he came home again and was very sad, for he wanted a true princess so very much.

One evening there was a terrible storm. The lightning flashed, the thunder boomed, and the rain poured down! It was really frightful! Then somebody knocked at the city gate, and the old king went out to open it.

A princess was standing outside, but heavens, how she looked from the rain and the bad weather! Water poured off her hair and clothes and ran in at the toe of her shoe and out at the heel, but she said she was a true princess!

'Well, we'll soon find that out!' thought the old queen, but she didn't say anything. She went into the bedroom, took off all the bedding, and put a pea on the bottom of the bed. Then she took twenty mattresses and laid them on top of the pea and then put twenty eiderdown quilts on top of the mattresses. There the princess was to sleep that night.

In the morning they asked her how she had slept.

'Oh, just miserably!' said the princess. 'I've hardly closed my eyes all night! Heaven knows what was in my bed! I've been lying on something so hard that I'm black and blue all over! It's simply dreadful!'

Then they could tell that this was a true princess, because through the twenty mattresses and the twenty eiderdown quilts she had felt the pea. Only a true princess could have such delicate skin.

So the prince took her for his wife, for now he knew that he had a true princess, and the pea was put into the museum, where it can still be seen, if no one has taken it!

See, this was a true story!

Word and sentence

- Make large signs for 'prince', 'princess', 'old king' and 'old queen'.
- Make large signs for 'storm', 'pea', and 'bed'. Children to make and label pictures of both.
- Counting to twenty. Each child to bring a small box to represent 'mattress'. Use thick pieces of fabric for 'quilts'. Children to stack them up in twenties.
- Draw their attention to: 'he', 'wanted', 'true', 'went', 'find out', 'very sad', 'she', 'bad', 'off', 'her', 'put', 'on top', 'sleep', and 'hard'. Write in alphabetical order on a poster with drawings by the children.
- Children to say whenever they can recognise a word in the large copy of the story.
- Write these sentences in big letters on strips of paper and display: 'There was once a prince.'; 'It was really frightful!'; '"Well, we'll soon find that out!"'; 'There the princess was to sleep that night.'; '"Heaven knows what was in my bed!"'; 'Only a true princess could have such delicate skin.', and 'See, this was a true story!'
- Children to say when they recognise these sentences and point them out.
- Draw attention to capital letters and full stops. Can the children spot other special marks?

Reading

- Children to:
  1. Imagine and describe the 'true princess' arriving at the city gate.
  2. Imagine her first night's sleep in the palace. What was it like? How did she feel?
  3. Share stories about having a bad night's sleep.

- Children to draw pictures of:
  1. prince 'journeying all around the world';
  2. prince looking sad at home;
  3. princess arriving at the gate;
  4. old king letting her in;
  5. old queen making up the bed;
  6. princess sleeping in it;
  7. princess telling them how uncomfortable it was;
  8. prince and princess getting married.
- Children to number the pictures 1 to 8 and label them with phrases from the text such as 'All around the world' for 1., 'Very sad' for 2. and so on.
- Use the sets of pictures as a storyboard to be put in order by the children.

Writing

- Pairs to work out new stories based on this one:
  1. Where the princess came from.
  2. What the prince and princess's son/daughter did.
  3. A magic bird comes to the palace.

Dance, drama and music

- In the school hall play the following games:
  1. Searching for the 'true princess'. Individually, the children go journeying. How do they travel? By horse, by car, by ship, by air, in a rocket? Where do they go to? What is the place like, where they find their princess? Pair the children – boy/girl – if possible. The girls are to imagine what they would be doing as a princess while the boys journey. Why are they not 'true' princesses? What is the 'something that wasn't quite right'?
  2. Making the storm. How can they show the 'lightning flashing', the thunder that 'boomed' and the rain that 'poured down'. Children also to use percussion instruments for this.
  3. Sleeping in an uncomfortable bed. Children lie down and invent different ways of being uncomfortable in bed. What would they say to themselves in the night? What would they say to someone else next morning?
- Group the children in fours to re-enact the scene in which the old queen makes up the bed, the princess sleeps in it and the meeting between princess, prince, old queen and old king next morning.

Art

- Children to paint their favourite part or character in the story.

Y1: T3. A. A. Milne, **Pooh Invents a New Game**[12]

Text

1. Now one day Pooh and Piglet and Rabbit and Roo were all playing Poohsticks together. They had dropped their sticks in when Rabbit said, 'Go!' and they had hurried across to the other side of the bridge, and now they were all leaning over the edge, waiting to see whose stick would come out first. But it was a long time coming, because the river was very lazy that day, and hardly seemed to mind if it didn't ever get there at all.

   'I can see mine!' cried Roo. 'No, I can't. It's something else. Can you see yours, Piglet? I thought I could see mine, but I couldn't. There it is! No, it isn't. Can you see yours, Pooh?'

   'No,' said Pooh.

   'I expect my stick's stuck,' said Roo.

   'Rabbit, my stick's stuck. Is your stick stuck, Piglet?'

   'They always take longer than you think,' said Rabbit.

   'How long do you *think* they'll take? ' asked Roo.

   'I can see yours, Piglet,' said Pooh suddenly.

   'Mine's a sort of greyish one,' said Piglet, not daring to lean too far over in case he fell in.

   'Yes, that's what I can see. It's coming over my side.'

   Rabbit leant over further than ever, looking for his and Roo wriggled up and down, calling out 'Come on stick! Stick, stick, stick!' and Piglet got very excited because his was the only one which had been seen, and that meant he was winning.

   'It's coming!' said Pooh.

   'Are you sure it's mine?' squeaked Piglet excitedly.

   'Yes, because it's grey. A big grey one. Here it comes! A very – big – grey – Oh, no, it isn't, it's Eeyore.'

   And out floated Eeyore. (pages 10 to 12)

2. 'And where was Tigger?' asked Rabbit.

   Before Eeyore could answer, there was a loud noise behind them, and through the hedge came Tigger himself.

   'Hallo, everybody,' said Tigger cheerfully.

   'Hallo, Tigger,' said Roo.

   Rabbit became very important suddenly.

   'Tigger,' he said solemnly, 'what happened just now?'

   'Just when?' said Tigger a little uncomfortably.

   'When you bounced Eeyore into the river.'

   'I didn't bounce him.'

   'You bounced me,' said Eeyore gruffly.

   'I didn't really. I have a cough, and I happened to be behind Eeyore, and I said "*Grrrr-opppp-ptschschschz*".'

   'Why?' said Rabbit, helping Piglet up, and dusting him. 'It's all right, Piglet.'

   'It took me by surprise,' said Piglet nervously.

   'That's what I call bouncing,' said Eeyore. (page 23)

Word and sentence

1.
- Write *ay* – 'day', *ey* – 'greyish', 'grey', *oo* – 'Pooh', 'Roo', *ck* – 'stick', 'stuck' on flipchart;
- Children to find these in the passage and provide other examples, reciting the sounds and words frequently.

2.
- Write *ee* – 'Eeyore', 'cheerfully', *ou* – 'loud', 'bounced' on flipchart.
- Children to:
  1. Look for double letter spelling patterns: e.g. 'Tigger', 'Eeyore', 'Hallo', 'little' and list them.
  2. Practise speaking words with single and double letters, trying to show sound difference.

Reading

- Pairs to discuss how to play Pooh sticks. Discuss as a class.
- Do they have any interesting games? What are the rules?
- Children to work out simple statements about the characters Pooh, Roo, Eeyore, Rabbit, and Tigger: e.g. 'Roo is a young kangaroo'. Develop further as follows: read pages 11 and 12 which show that Roo has a lot to say, then ask 'What else can you say about Roo?'
- Pairs to decide the most important things in each episode and record – with help.

Writing

- Children to write favourite parts of the story in their own words and to write reasons why they like them best. Use scribes to help.
- Pairs to make up their own Pooh story, orally at first, then tell it to others, then write it.

Dance and drama

- Children to find ways of moving like the various characters and to compare them: e.g. how Tigger would look and move, compared to Eeyore. Involve them in continual discussion about this.
- Develop recitations through mime then use the text as a script and make playlets.
- If possible, take the children to a bridge over a stream and play real Poohsticks!

Art

- Children to:
  1. copy Sheppard's paintings of the characters
  2. work out their own paintings of the locations in which the action takes place, either from drawings from direct observation or imagination.

Music

● Children to make sound pictures, using percussion instruments, their own voices and bodies, of:
  1. Eeyore in the river going round and round;
  2. Eeyore being 'bounced' or coughed at by Tigger then falling in the stream.

Y2: T3. Oscar Wilde, *'The Selfish Giant'*[13]

Text

1. Every afternoon, as they were coming home from school, the children used to go and play in the Giant's garden.

   It was a large lovely garden, with soft green grass. Here and there over the grass stood beautiful flowers like stars, and there were twelve peach trees that in the spring-time broke out into delicate blossoms of pink and pearl, and in the autumn bore rich fruit. The birds sat on the trees and sang so sweetly that the children used to stop their games in order to listen to them. 'How happy we are here!' they cried to each other.

   One day the Giant came back. He had been to visit his friend the Cornish ogre, and had stayed with him for seven years. After the seven years were over he had said all that he had to say, for his conversation was limited, and he determined to return to his own castle. When he arrived he saw the children playing in the garden.

   'What are you doing here?' he cried in a very gruff voice, and the children ran away.

   'My own garden is my own garden,' said the Giant; 'anyone can understand that, and I will allow nobody to play in it but myself.' So he built a high wall all round it, and put up a notice board. 'Trespassers will be prosecuted.'

   He was a very selfish giant. (p.27)

2. 'I cannot understand why the Spring is so late in coming,' said the Selfish Giant, as he sat at the window and looked out at his cold, white garden; 'I hope there will be a change in the weather.'

   But the Spring never came, nor the Summer. The Autumn gave golden fruit to every garden, but to the Giant's garden she gave none. 'He is too selfish,' she said. So it was always winter there, and the North Wind and the Hail, and the Frost, and the Snow danced about through the trees.

   One morning the Giant was lying awake in bed when he heard some lovely music. It sounded so sweet to his ears that he thought it must be the King's musicians passing by. It was really only a little linnet singing outside his window, but it was so long since he had heard a bird in his garden that it seemed to him to be the most beautiful music in the world. Then the Hail stopped dancing over his head, and the North Wind ceased roaring, and a delicious perfume came to him through the open casement. 'I believe the Spring has come at last,' said the Giant; and he jumped out of bed and looked out.

   What did he see?

He saw the most beautiful sight. Through a little hole in the wall the children had crept in, and they were sitting in the branches of the trees. In every tree that he could see there was a little child. And the trees were so glad to have the children back again that they had covered themselves with blossoms, and were waving their arms gently above the children's heads. (pages 29 to 30)

Word and sentence

1.
- Write *oo* – 'afternoon', 'school'; *ee* – 'green', 'trees', 'sweetly', 'been'; *ow* – 'flowers', 'How', 'allow' on flipchart. Children to find them in the extract.
- Focus on 'ogre'. What other monster words can they find? Make a list. Children to draw and paint them according to the descriptions they find.
- Draw attention to spelling of 'gruff'. What other words do they know with that sound? How are they spelt? Make a chart of -*uff* words and -*ough* words.
- Children to consider and discuss what 'Trespassers will be prosecuted' means?

2.
- Write *ou* – 'sounded', 'outside' (compare with *ow*); *ough* – 'Through' (compare with *ough* above); *ai* – 'Hail' on flipchart. Children to find in the extract and further examples.
- Write the three sentences which the Giant speaks.
- Groups to make these statements into questions: e.g. 'I hope there will be a change in the weather' – 'Will there be a change in the weather?'

Reading

- When reading the story, break off on 'What did he see?' (when spring comes to the garden). Children to imagine what he sees and predict what will happen next.
- Children to:
  1. find out all they can about Oscar Wilde, using book covers, encyclopaedias and CD-Rom and to share it.
  2. share other giant stories they know and say how they are different from Oscar Wilde's.
  3. either read other stories by Oscar Wilde to compare with 'The Selfish Giant', or
  4. read and compare a variety of other giant stories.

Writing

- Children to prepare to write a giant story as follows:
  1. What sort of giant? What does he look like? What things does he do? Will he have a catch-phrase like 'Fee, fi, fo, fum'? Is he good, bad or a mixture like Oscar Wilde's giant?
  2. What other characters will be in it?
  3. Where will the story take place?

- Children to make up their stories orally as follows:
  1. Close eyes and think about the giant, living where he lives, and the other characters.
  2. What happens first? What does your giant do? What happens to your giant?
  3. What happens next? Take it on from there.
  4. Children to imagine a sequence of events.
  5. When they have a story in their heads, they should tell it to a partner.
- Children to write their stories with following guidelines:
  1. Describe the giant, the other characters and the place where the story happens.
  2. Put words into the characters' mouths.
  3. Keep it going. (Allow time for this.)

Dance and drama

- Children to imitate the giant when:
  1. he speaks gruffly
  2. when he is friendly
  3. when he is outraged at the treatment of the boy
  4. when he is sad.
- Children to consider
  1. How would he hold himself?
  2. How would he walk?
  3. What gestures might he make?
- Children to build a Selfish Giant sequence from being gruff to being kind.
- Explore what Spring, Summer, Autumn and Winter look like, move like and behave like. How would Autumn say, 'He is too selfish'? If the other seasons said something what would it be and how would they say it?
- Explore how The North Wind, the Hail, the Frost and the Snow each 'danced about through the trees'.
- Develop children's movements into dances with costumes or pieces of fabric in hands.
- Children to make words for these weathers to speak or sounds for them to make.
- Groups to improvise the encounters in the story.
- Build a dramatic performance for an audience.

Music

- Use music to support the dances as follows:
  1. Pre-recorded, ensure that children know the composer's name, origin and time.
  2. Composed on simple instruments by the children, with time to explore instruments, including voices and bodies.
- Explore the contrasts though this work: gruff–gentle, warm–cold, soft–harsh, kind–unkind.

Art

- Show paintings of gardens from great painters e.g. Monet's garden, as follows:
  1. Children discuss what they see.
  2. Tell them that it shows the impression you see when you first look at the garden.
- Children to:
  1. Explore the text for descriptions of the garden in the different seasons: e.g. for spring we get a description of green grass, flowers like stars and peach trees in blossom.
  2. Decide which season to paint the Giant's garden in.
  3. Copy the descriptions in the story.
  4. Sit and imagine it.
  5. Sketch basic features they want in their paintings.
  6. Mix the colours they will need.
  7. Paint their gardens.
  8. When they are finished – perhaps – put characters into them.

Y3: T3. L. Frank Baum, The Wizard of Oz[14]

Text

1. The little old woman took the slate from her nose, and having read the words on it, asked, 'Is your name Dorothy, my dear?'

   'Yes,' answered the child, looking up and drying her tears.

   'Then you must go to the City of Emeralds. Perhaps Oz will help you.'

   'Where is this city?' asked Dorothy.

   'It is exactly in the center of the country, and is ruled by Oz, the Great Wizard I told you of.'

   'Is he a good man?' inquired the girl anxiously.

   'He is a good Wizard. Whether he is a man or not I cannot tell, for I have never seen him.'

   'How can I get there?' asked Dorothy.

   'You must walk. It is a long journey, through a country that is sometimes pleasant and sometimes dark and terrible. However, I will use all the magic arts I know of to keep you from harm.'

   'Won't you go with me?' pleaded the girl, who had begun to look upon the little old woman as her only friend.

   'No, I cannot do that,' she replied, 'but I will give you a kiss, and no one will dare injure a person who has been kissed by the Witch of the North.'

   She came close to Dorothy and kissed her gently on the forehead. Where her lips touched the girl they left a round, shining mark, as Dorothy found out soon after.

   'The road to the City of Emeralds is paved with yellow brick,' said the Witch, 'so you cannot miss it. When you get to Oz do not be afraid of him, but tell your story and ask him to help you. Good-bye, my dear.' (Pages 14 to 15)

2. 'Just to amuse myself, and keep the good people busy, I ordered them to build this City, and my Palace; and they did it willingly and well. Then I thought, as the country was so green and beautiful, I would call it the Emerald City, and to make the name fit better I put green spectacles on all the people, so that everything they saw was green.'

'But isn't everything here green?' asked Dorothy.

'No more than in any other city,' replied Oz; 'but when you wear green spectacles, why of course everything you see looks green to you. The Emerald City was built a great many years ago, for I was a young man when the balloon brought me here, and I am a very old man now. But my people have worn green glasses on their eyes so long that most of them think it really is an Emerald City, and it certainly is a beautiful place, abounding in jewels and precious metals, and every good thing that is needed to make one happy. I have been good to the people, and they like me; but ever since this Palace was built I have shut myself up and would not see any of them.

'One of my greatest fears was the Witches, for while I had no magic powers at all I soon found out that the Witches were really able to do wonderful things. There were four of them in this country, and they ruled the people who live in the North and South and East and West. Fortunately, the Witches of the North and South were good, and I knew they would do me no harm; but the Witches of the East and West were terribly wicked, and had they not thought I was more powerful than they themselves, they would surely have destroyed me. As it was, I lived in deadly fear of them for many years; so you can imagine how pleased I was when I heard your house had fallen on the Wicked Witch of the East. When you came to me I was willing to promise anything if you would only do away with the other Witch; but, now that you have melted her, I am ashamed to say that I cannot keep my promises.'

'I think you are a very bad man,' said Dorothy.

'Oh, no, my dear; I'm really a very good man; but I'm a very bad Wizard, I must admit.'

'Can't you give me brains?' asked the Scarecrow.

'You don't need them. You are learning something every day. A baby has brains, but it doesn't know much. Experience is the only thing that brings knowledge, and the longer you are on earth the more experience you are sure to get.' (Pages 138 to 140)

Word and sentence

1.

- Write *ou*: 'country', 'touched' and *our*; 'journey' on flipchart, ask for further examples and examples of other sounds *ou* can make.
- Write *ow*: 'out', 'shout' and *ought*: 'bought' and 'fought' with other examples on flipchart.
- Revise pronouns: words that stand for nouns or names.
- Groups to:
  1. List nouns which *it* stands for ('slate', 'city'), *he* stands for ('Wizard') and *she* stands for ('little old woman').
  2. Investigate whether or not Dorothy is represented by a pronoun. If not, how is Dorothy represented when not named ('the child', 'the girl')?

2.

- Consider ways that the *i* sound is made, as in 'busy', 'build', 'did'.
- Children to find the examples and list on flipchart.
- Consider the soft and hard *c* sounds as in 'city' and 'country' and the soft and hard *g* sounds, as in 'magic' and 'good'.
- Children to list examples.
- Children to:
  1. Work out meanings of 'abounding' and 'experience' using the context.
  2. Investigate use of speech marks and other speech punctuation: where are the questions?
  3. Find where commas go when a piece of speech is stopped part way through, e.g. 'No more than in any other city,' replied Oz.
- Groups to investigate how the author conveys the passage of time at the beginning of Chapters 4, 5, 6 and 10. How do they show the passage of time in their own stories? Children to compile lists of phrases which can be used.

Reading

- At various stages of the story ask the children who is actually telling it. Usually, it is told directly by the author in the third person. However, some parts of the story are told by characters: e.g. most of Extract 2 is told by the Wizard of Oz in the first person.
- Establish the difference between the two ways the author uses to tell a story and teach the children that 'first Person' is about 'I', 'Me', 'We' and 'Us' and that 'third Person' is about 'He', 'Him', 'She', 'Her', 'They' and Them'.
- After Chapter 14, children to decide which part they find most exciting or frightening and which words, phrases and sentences create this. Children to write short summaries.
- Groups to discuss the following issues when they are raised in the story:
  1. Chapter 4: Why should Dorothy 'wish to leave this beautiful country' to return to 'the dry, gray place' called Kansas?
  2. Chapter 5: Is it more important to have good brains for working things out or a good heart for feelings?
  3. Chapter 6: What makes a coward and what makes a brave person?
  4. Chapter 7: Does the Scarecrow behave as if he has no brains?
  5. Chapter 8: Does the Lion behave as if he has no courage?
  6. Chapter 9: Does the Tin Woodman behave as if he is heartless?
- Children to build character logs as follows:
  1. make a first impressions judgment
  2. add notes as the characters reveal more about themselves
  3. include a balance of facts and opinions.

Writing

- Children to:
  1. Write overview of the character they have been logging at the end of the story.
  2. Describe favourite incident, write why they liked it and the main sentences in it.
  3. Choose one of the discussion topics and write their own arguments about it.

   4. Pretend they are one of the characters and describe an incident from that point of view.

- Children to invent their own imaginary country for Dorothy and her friends to go to and to plan an extended story about it as follows:
  1. Work out the main feature or theme of the place, e.g. China Country made of brittle China which affects everything else.
  2. Invent and describe new characters and how they will behave.
  3. Make up incidents involving Dorothy and friends.
  4. Write detailed descriptions for key parts.

Dance and drama

- Children to imitate the spinning motion of the cyclone, developing ways of controlling these actions, e.g. slow motion.
- Pairs to develop spinning actions further by showing the stillness in the vortex and the cyclone picking up, carrying and placing Dorothy somewhere else.
- Groups to take this idea further.
- Children to imitate and contrast the movements the characters make, e.g. Scarecrow and Tin Woodman. Distinctly different movement motifs to be made for each character.
- When about half way through the book groups to work on an encounter as follows:
  1. Read the passage to reflect punctuation and the variations of voice between the narrator (author) and the characters, showing the different characters in their voices.
  2. Retell the story in their own words, taking turns.
  3. Improvise the incident with actions and words, taking parts.
  4. Develop the improvisations by including the characters' actual words.
  5. Rehearse 3. or 4. for a performance.
  6. Repeat with an incident from the second half of the book.

Music

- Children to:
  1. Develop signature tunes for the main characters, as in Chapter 3, 'Art and music'.
  2. Make compositions for the four witches to demonstrate what they are like, where they come from and what happens to them in the end.

Art

- Children to make:
  1. portraits of the characters, using descriptions in the text;
  2. landscapes, using the descriptions of the various countries, including that of Kansas;
  3. murals, using the Road of Yellow Brick as a central motif and which children add to as the story progresses;
  4. 3D Monsters, by either sculpting in clay or papier mâché and wire mesh of the various weird beasts.

Y4: T1. *Frances Hodgson Burnett,* **The Secret Garden**[15]

Text

1. It was a very strange thing indeed. She quite caught her breath when she stopped to look at it. A boy was sitting under a tree, with his back against it, playing on a rough wooden pipe. He was a funny-looking boy about twelve. He looked very clean and his nose turned up and his cheeks were as red as poppies, and never had Mistress Mary seen such round and such blue eyes in any boy's face. And on the trunk of the tree he leaned against, a brown squirrel was clinging and watching him, and from behind a bush near by a cock pheasant was delicately stretching his neck to peep out, and quite near him were two rabbits sitting up and sniffing with tremulous noses – and actually it appeared as if they were all drawing near to watch him and listen to the strange, low, little call his pipe seemed to make.

    When he saw Mary he held up his hand and spoke to her in a voice almost as low as and rather like his piping.

    'Don't tha' move,' he said. 'It'd flight 'em.'

    Mary remained motionless. He stopped playing his pipe and began to rise from the ground. He moved so slowly that it scarcely seemed as though he were moving at all, but at last he stood on his feet and then the squirrel scampered back up into the branches of his tree, the pheasant withdrew his head, and the rabbits dropped on all fours and began to hop away, though not at all as if they were frightened.

    'I'm Dickon,' the boy said. 'I know th'rt Mary.' (Pages 79 to 80)

2. 'Have you – do you think you have found out anything at all about the way into the secret garden?'

    Mary looked at his poor little tired face and swollen eyes and her heart relented.

    'Ye-es,' she answered. 'I think I have. And if you will go to sleep I will tell you tomorrow.'

    His hand quite trembled.

    'Oh, Mary!' he said. 'Oh, Mary! If I could go into it I think I should live to grow up! Do you suppose that instead of singing the Ayah song – you could just tell me softly as you did that first day what you imagine it looks like inside? I am sure it will make me go to sleep.'

    'Yes,' answered Mary. 'Shut your eyes.'

    He closed his eyes and lay quite still and she held his hand and began to speak very slowly and in a very low voice.

    'I think it has been left alone so long – that it has grown all into a lovely tangle. I think the roses have climbed and climbed and climbed until they hang from the branches and walls and creep along the ground – almost like a strange grey mist. Some of them have died, but many – are alive, and when the summer comes there will be curtains and fountains of roses. I think the ground is full of daffodils and snowdrops and lilies and iris working their way out of the dark. Now the spring has begun – perhaps – perhaps –'

    The soft drone of her voice was making him stiller and stiller, and she saw it and went on.

'Perhaps they are coming up through the grass – perhaps there are clusters of purple crocuses and gold ones – even now. Perhaps the leaves are beginning to break out and uncurl – and perhaps – the grey is changing and a green gauze veil is creeping – and creeping over – everything. And the birds are coming to look at it – because it is – safe and still. And perhaps – perhaps – perhaps' very softly and slowly indeed, 'the robin has found a mate – and is building a nest.'

And Colin was asleep. (pages 146 to 147)

Alterations to the text

- For a flowing narrative replace the following with storytelling:
  1. Pages 216, 217 and the first eight lines of page 218.
  2. Page 225 and the first 16 lines of page 226.
- To eliminate racist overtones do the following:
  1. Say the story was written when Britain ruled an Empire of many countries overseas and one was India and that attitudes towards Indian people were racist and unacceptable.
  2. Say that Mary's words on page 28 show bad attitudes inherited from her parents.
  3. Cut all use of the words 'native', 'blacks' and 'heathens'.

Word and sentence

1.
- Write *ou*: 'round', 'ground'; *ow*: 'brown' on flipchart with further examples and compare.
- Write *ea*: 'leaned', 'near', 'appeared'; *ee*; 'tree', 'seemed', 'feet' and compare.
- Children to work out the meanings from context and inference of: 'delicately', 'tremulous', motionless', 'scarcely', 'scampered' and check by looking in the dictionary.

2.
- Teach verb 'tense': something is done in the past, present or future.
- Children to work out which tenses we usually use when
  1. we tell a story (past)
  2. describing what we are doing (present)
  3. we say what we intend to do (future).
- Children to find and copy examples of the past tense in the extract.
- Children to investigate the different words used for 'grow' or 'growing': e.g. 'coming up', 'break out', 'uncurl', 'changing' and 'creeping'.

Reading

- Groups to investigate how we get to know what characters are like by the details in their descriptions, thoughts and actions: e.g. we know that Colin is an unhappy boy because of the strange cries Mary hears. Groups to choose one of Mary, Dickon, Colin, Mrs Medlock and Martha, looking for and recording details of:

1. author's description
2. thoughts or attitudes
3. things they do.

- After Chapter 16 children to predict what will happen to the characters. Will they:
  1. be as they are now and remain in the same circumstances?
  2. change in some way and have different expectations?
- Groups to investigate how we get to know what Mary's house in India and Misselthwaite Manor are like by the details in their descriptions: e.g. we know that Misselthwaite Manor is a remote place by the descriptions of the moors in Chapter 20.
- Pairs to work out how much time has passed from the beginning to the end of the story, looking in two chapters each for evidence of the passage of time.
- Groups to work out and record the main stages of the story, identifying:
  1. The main conflicts or dramatic events, e.g. cholera epidemic.
  2. When is it first obvious that the conflict/event might happen? e.g. when Mary's usual servant is not available.
  3. How is the conflict/event resolved? e.g. Mary rescued and taken to England.

Writing

- Using their notes from the investigations into characters children to write an evaluation of their character at the end of Chapter 14 to be reviewed with additional paragraphs at the end.
- Children to list main characteristics of their characters. Discuss as a class.
- Groups to turn one chapter into a play for voices following the suggestions in Chapter 3, 'Scripted Plays'.
- Using notes from the work on main stages of the story, children to imagine and write how they would respond to a situation. e.g. what would they have done when the cholera epidemic broke out?
- Children to make up and write their own stories with the following process:
  1. On a large piece of paper either to write notes, draw sketches or symbols to represent what they imagine in a brainstorm about a secret place.
  2. Close eyes and imagine the secret place, a place they already know or a place of pure invention. How it is concealed? What incident might lead to its discovery?
  3. They should really try to see it. Their first impressions What they find as they walk about in it
  4. Who might they share this place with? What sort of things would they do in there? Would the secret be shared by anyone else other than them?
  5. Use notes to tell another person the story, making it up as they go along and asking for responses from each other.
  6. When they have told the story they should write it, bearing in mind how characters and settings are built by the little details in their descriptions and paying attention to how a dramatic incident is more effectively developed if it is introduced, built up to a climax and resolved or sorted out.

Drama and music

● Children to have ample opportunity to rehearse and improve their play scripts. When they have reached a good standard of voice production, sound effects and music through this process of rehearsal, they should record their plays.

Art

● Children to:
   1. Either respond to their own stories about secret places, particularly the descriptions they make of the place itself, with a large drawing, painting, model or sculpture. They should decide how best this can be done then make initial drawings in their sketchbooks.
   2. Or make a series of illustrations to show key moments in their stories.

Y5: T2. Henry Wadsworth Longfellow, The Song of Hiawatha[16]

Text

1. How Hiawatha's grandmother, old Nokomis, brings him up and teaches him some of the tribe's beliefs and how Hiawatha befriends the birds and animals.

By the shores of Gitchee Gumee,
By the shining Big-Sea-Water,
Stood the wigwam of Nokomis,
Daughter of the moon, Nokomis.
Dark behind it rose the forest,
Rose the black and gloomy pine-trees,
Rose the firs with cones upon them;
Bright before it beat the water,
Beat the clear and sunny water,
Beat the shining Big-Sea-Water.
    There the wrinkled, old Nokomis
Nursed the little Hiawatha,
Rocked him in his linden cradle,
Bedded soft in moss and rushes,
Safely bound with reindeer sinews;
Stilled his fretful wail by saying,
'Hush! the Naked Bear will hear thee!'
Lulled him into slumber, singing,
'Ewa-yea! my little owlet!
Who is this that lights the wigwam?
With his great eyes lights the wigwam?
Ewa-yea! my little owlet!'
    Many things Nokomis taught him
Of the stars that shine in heaven;
Showed him Ishkoodah, the comet,
Ishkoodah with fiery tresses;
Showed the Death-Dance of the spirits,

Warriors with their plumes and war-clubs,
Flaring far away to northward
In the frosty nights of Winter;
Showed the broad, white road in heaven,
Pathway of the ghosts, the shadows,
Running straight across the heavens,
Crowded with the ghost, the shadows.
   At the door on summer evenings
Sat the little Hiawatha:
Heard the whispering of the pine-trees,
Heard the lapping of the water,
Sounds of music, words of wonder;
'Minne-wawa!' said the pine-trees,
'Mudway-aushka!' said the water.
   Saw the firefly, Wah-wah-taysee,
Flitting through the dusk at evening,
With the twinkle of its candle
Lighting up the brakes and bushes;
And he sang the song of children,
Sang the song Nokomis taught him:
'Wah-way-taysee, little firefly,
Little flitting, white-fire insect,
Little dancing, white-fire creature,
Light me with your little candle,
Ere upon my bed I lay me,
Ere in sleep I close my eyelids!'
   Saw the moon rise from the water
Rippling, rounding from the water,
Saw the flecks and shadows on it,
Whispered: 'What is that, Nokomis?'
And the good Nokomis answered:
'Once a warrior, very angry,
Seized his grandmother, and threw her
Up into the sky at midnight;
Right against the moon he threw her;
'Tis her body that you see there.'
   Saw the rainbow in the heaven,
In the eastern sky the rainbow,
Whispered: 'What is that Nokomis?'
And the good Nokomis answered:
'Tis the heaven of flowers you see there:
All the wild flowers of the forest,
All the lilies of the prairie,
When on earth they fade and perish,
Blossom in that heaven above us.'
   When he heard the owls at midnight,
Hooting, laughing in the forest,
'What is that?' he cried in terror;
'What is that,' he said, 'Nokomis?'

And the good Nokomis answered:
'That is but the owl and owlet,
Talking in their native language,
Talking, scolding at each other.'
   Then the little Hiawatha
Learned of every bird its language,
Learned their names and all their secrets,
How they built their nests in Summer,
Where they hid themselves in Winter,
Talked with them when'er he met them,
Called them 'Hiawatha's Chickens'.
   Of all beasts he learned the language,
Learned their names and all their secrets,
How the beavers built their lodges,
Where the squirrels hid their acorns,
How the reindeer ran so swiftly,
Why the rabbit was so timid,
Talked to them when'er he met them,
Called them 'Hiawatha's brothers'. (from Book Three)

2. How the villainous Pau-Puk-Keewis insults Hiawatha by killing some of his friends, the birds, and ransacks his home. He comes across Hiawatha's home and sees it is empty.

'All are gone! the lodge is empty!'
Thus it was spake Pau-Puk-Keewis,
In his heart resolving mischief;
'Gone is wary Hiawatha,
Gone the silly Laughing Water,
Gone Nokomis, the old woman,
And the lodge is left unguarded.
   By the neck he seized the raven,
Whirled it round him like a rattle,
Like a medicine-pouch he shook it,
Strangled Kahgahkee, the raven,
From the ridge-pole of the wigwam
Left its lifeless body hanging,
As an insult to its master,
As a taunt to Hiawatha.
   With a stealthy step he entered,
Round the lodge in wild disorder
Threw the household things about him,
Piled together in confusion
Bowls of wood and earthen kettles,
Robes of buffalo and beaver,
Skins of otter, lynx and ermine,
As an insult to Nokomis,
As a taunt to Minnehaha.
   Then departed Pau-Puk-Keewis,
Whistling, singing through the forest,

Whistling gaily to the squirrels,
Who from hollow boughs above him
Dropped their acorn-shells upon him,
Singing gaily to the wood-birds,
Who from out the leafy darkness
Answered with a song as merry.
   Then he climbed the rocky headlands,
Looking o'er the Gitchee Gumee,
Perched himself upon their summit,
Waiting full of mirth and mischief
The return of Hiawatha.
   Stretched upon his back he lay there;
Far below him plashed the waters,
Plashed and washed the dreamy waters;
Far above him swam the heavens,
Swam the dizzy, dreamy heavens;
Round him hovered, fluttered, rustled,
Hiawatha's mountain chickens,
Flock-wise swept and wheeled about him,
Almost brushed him with their pinions.
   And he killed them as he lay there,
Slaughtered them by tens and twenties,
Threw their bodies down the headland,
Threw them on the beach below him,
Till at length Kayoshk, the sea-gull,
Perched upon a crag above them,
Shouted: 'It is Pau-Puk-Keewis!
He is slaying us by hundreds!
Send a message to our brother,
Tidings send to Hiawatha!'
(from Book 16)

Preparing the work

- Cut the Prologue and Books I and II and summarise them at the beginning of the project.
- Read Books III to XI.
- Cut Books XII to XV and summarise them.
- Read Books XV to XVII.
- Cut Books XVII to XXII and summarise them.
- Leave the end of the story in the air to provide opportunity for new Hiawatha stories.

Word and sentence

- Groups to read passages of text, ensuring that the rhythm is maintained throughout, attempting to change their voices to suit the different characters who are speaking and paying special attention to the role of the comma: e.g. in 'Crowded with the ghosts, the shadows' there should be a slight but definite pause after 'ghosts'.

1.

- Write on flipchart: 'bedded', 'running' and 'flitting' as words with double letters which come from roots with single letters: 'bed', 'run' and 'flit'. Children to add others.
- Teach onomatopoeia as a word which sounds like the thing it means. e.g. 'lapping'; 'wail', 'Hooting'. Children to search and add to list.

2.

- Revise pronouns as short words that stand for somebody or something: e.g. 'he' stands for Pau-Puk Keewis and 'it' stands for the raven.
- Groups to look for pronouns, list them and write who or what each stands for.

Reading

- Tell the children that the stories in *The Song of Hiawatha* were not 'made up' by Longfellow, but that he collected them from Native Americans and wove them together in his own way. Tell them that the stories were originally told, probably around campfires and not written, that Longfellow wrote them in this particular way – as a long narrative poem – with a strong Native American rhythm like drumbeats.
- Groups to follow up retellings of each episode with discussion of what it is about, deciding how much is plain narrative and how much is description.
- Children to write examples of plain narrative and of description and decide why the description is there.
- Children to discuss the following:
  1. In what ways are the people in the story different from ourselves in their beliefs, habits, dress, the way they treat each other and their entertainments?
  2. Could any episode be told differently to make a good character not so good and a bad character not so bad?
  3. Compare the way this story is told with the way other stories are told.
- At the halfway stage of the project (end of Book VIII) allocate a book to each group with the following tasks:
  1. Read aloud a favourite part of the story.
  2. Tell that part of the story.
- The groups to perform the two versions to the whole class then discuss the differences between them.

Writing

- Children to research, plan, write, review and edit their own legends as follows:
  1. Find a legend, learn it and practise telling it to friends and family.
  2. Divide the story into sections: chapters, verses or, even, books as in Longfellow's work.
  3. Decide on a 'voice' or viewpoint: autobiographical in the first person or as an author in the third person.
  4. Decide on a style: in imitation of 'The Song of Hiawatha' or in prose.
  5. Write the story and, when finished, read it through.

6. Ask friends to read it and make comments.
7. Using dictionaries and thesauruses, check it for content, quality of language and correctness.
8. Produce a final form and share it with others.

Music, dance and drama

- Children to:
  1. Count the number of beats or syllables in different lines to establish the pattern and clap the rhythm.
  2. Make this rhythm with non-pitched musical instruments, particularly ones with skins and to work on it until it is right, then experiment with one and two beats for a phrase playing alongside the full four beats.
  3. Play these rhythms alongside readings of the lines.
  4. Beat out these rhythms on parts of their bodies: chest, thighs, head, feet, knees, any part suitable; then on the floor of the school hall with their hand.
  5. Beat the rhythm on the floor with their feet and move around in various directions.
- Children to explore gestures: e.g. show Hiawatha returning in triumph with the Wampum.
- Establish sequences in which the children walk – pause – make a gesture slowly and exaggeratedly – walk. Develop this basic technique along the following lines:
  1. Children in pairs walk – pause near each other – one makes a gesture, the other makes one in response – walk. Practise this.
  2. Establish a common set of gestures to represent common actions in the story, e.g. going somewhere far away shown with a long, raised arm and pointing finger.
- Groups to build a performance piece by:
  1. Telling the story through a series of movements and gestures which flow together.
  2. Working out music for these mimes, using bodies, voices and non-pitched instruments.
  3. Rehearsing and performing the mimes as a sequence linked with interludes of the rhythm dances accompanied by the beating on instruments.
  4. Introducing each scene with a summary of what happens in it.

Art

- Provide pictures of the following chief Native American art forms:
  1. Painted faces and masks, with masks made out of skins, wood and woven reeds, grass and woollen fabrics.
  2. Paintings on rock, skins, pottery and the human body.
  3. Woven cloth (for clothes), rugs, baskets, bags, wall-hangings and jewellery.
  4. Carvings in wood, stone and bone.[17]
- Children to spend time copying patterns, figures and other motifs from the pictures into their sketchbooks.
- Base art work on providing the dance, mime and music work, designing and making:

1. masks to represent the characters in the mimes
2. face decorations as an alternative to the masks
3. jewellery using string and packets of beads
4. headdresses by adding feathers to beaded headbands
5. dresses or shifts for female characters.[18]

Y6: T1. *William Shakespeare,* **The Tempest**[19]

The following project is designed to complement a project on 'The Tempest' planned under 'Literacy Hour Lessons' in the companion volume *Teaching Poetry in the Primary School* but can also be used independently.[20]

Text

1. Prospero is telling Miranda how they both came to the island many years ago, how they were helped by the loyal Gonzalo and how, by good fortune, all Prospero's enemies have been brought to the island in the recent storm.

MIRANDA: How came we ashore?
PROSPERO: By providence divine.
  Some food we had, and some fresh water, that
  A noble Neapolitan, Gonzalo,
  Out of his charity, who being then appointed
  Master of this design, did give us, with
  Rich garments, linens, stuffs and necessaries,
  Which since have steadied much; so, of his gentleness
  Knowing I lov'd my books, he furnish'd me
  From mine own library with volumes that
  I prize above my dukedom.
MIRANDA: Would I might
  But ever see that man!
PROSPERO: Now I arise:
  Sit still, and hear the last of our sea-sorrow.
  Here in this island we arriv'd; and here
  Have I, thy schoolmaster, made thee more profit
  Than other princess' can, that have more time
  For vainer hours, and tutors not so careful.
MIRANDA: Heavens thank you for't! And now, I pray you, sir,
  For still 'tis beating in my mind, your reason
  For raising this sea-storm?
PROSPERO: Know thus far forth.
  By accident most strange, bountiful Fortune
  (Now my dear lady) hath mine enemies
  Brought to this shore; and by my prescience
  I find my zenith doth depend upon
  A most auspicious star, whose influence

If now I court not, but omit, my fortunes
Will ever after droop. Here cease more questions:
Thou art inclin'd to sleep; 'tis a good dulness,
And give it way; I know thou canst not choose.
                    (Miranda sleeps)
(Act I, Scene ii. Lines 158 to 186.)

2. Having met Ferdinand once and been impressed by him, Miranda does not think it
   right that he should carry logs, a punishment inflicted by her father, Prospero. She
   offers to carry the logs herself, but Ferdinand declines. They begin to declare their
   love for each other.

MIRANDA: Alas now, pray you,
   Work not so hard: I would the lightning had
   Burnt up the logs that you are enjoin'd to pile!
   Pray, set it down and rest you: when this burns,
   'Twill weep for having wearied you. My father
   Is hard at study; pray, now, rest yourself:
   He's safe for these three hours.
FERDINAND: O most dear mistress,
   The sun will set before I shall discharge
   What I must strive to do.
MIRANDA: If you'll sit down,
   I'll bear your logs the while: pray give me that;
   I'll carry it to the pile.
FERDINAND: No precious creature;
   I had rather crack my sinews, break my back,
   Than thou should such dishonour undergo,
   While I sit lazy by.
MIRANDA: It would become me
   As well as it does you: I should do it
   With much more ease; for my good will is to it,
   And yours it is against.
PROSPERO: Poor worm, thou art infected!
   This visitation shows it.
MIRANDA: You look wearily.
FERDINAND: No, noble mistress: 'tis fresh morning with me
   When you are by at night. I do beseech you,
   Chiefly that I might set it in my prayers,
   What's your name?
MIRANDA: Miranda. O my father,
   I have broke your hest to say so!
FERDINAND: Admir'd Miranda!
   Indeed the top of admiration! worth
   What's dearest to the world! Full many a lady

I have ey'd with best regard, and many a time
Th'harmony of their tongues hath no bondage
Brought my diligent ear: for several virtues
Have I lik'd several women; never any
With so full soul, but some defect in her
Did quarrel with the noblest grace she ow'd,
And put it to the foil: but you, O you
So perfect and so peerless, are created
Of every creature's best!

MIRANDA: I do not know
One of my sex; no woman's face remember
Save, from my glass, mine own; nor have I seen
More that I may call men than you, good friend,
And my dear father: how features are abroad,
I am skilless of; but, by my modesty,
The jewel of my dower, I would not wish
Any companion in the world but you;
Nor can imagination form a shape
Besides yourself, to like of. But I prattle
Something too wildly, and my father's precepts
I therein do forget.

(Act III, Scene i. Lines 15 to 59)

Preparing the work

- Follow a storytelling approach, reading key extracts of text as you go along.
- Use the structure of five acts with different scenes in each act, including every scene in your presentation of the story to the children.
- So, instead of saying 'Once upon a time' or reading from Leon Garfield's retelling, 'Far, far away, upon the shore of a strange island'[21], take the children straight to the heart of *The Tempest* by saying, 'A ship is in a storm. There is "a tempestuous noise" [from the stage directions]. On board the ship there is a king and a prince, a duke and some lords, a jester, a butler, the captain and the crew . . .'.
- Divide the work into twelve episodes, finishing each at a dramatic moment in the story.
- Familiarise the children with the names, relationships and status of all the main characters by making a wallchart which is always available.
- Children to learn the names, how to say them and who they are, before the first episode.
- Be prepared to ask questions and explain things about the story and the characters as you go along. e.g. in the second scene of Act 1, the relationship between Prospero, his brother Antonio (who stole his position) and the King of Naples, Alonso (who helped him), will need to be carefully explained, perhaps with the use of diagrams on your board.

Word and Sentence

1.

- Provide this glossary: 'providence divine', help from God; 'Master of this design', man in charge of sending Prospero away; 'furnish'd me', gave me; 'made thee more profit', taught you better; 'vainer hours', time spent in front of the mirror; 'bountiful Fortune', very good luck; 'prescience', knowledge of events before they happen; 'auspicious star', favourable influence; 'If now I court not', if I don't act upon.
- Groups to look at, copy and work out the meanings of the following old word forms: 'How came we . . . ?', 'necessaries', 'thy', 'thee', 'for't', "tis', 'thus', 'doth', 'Thou art'.

2.

- Provide this glossary: 'enjoin'd', ordered (by Prospero); 'discharge', carry out; 'dishonour', disrespect; 'broke your hest', disobeyed you; 'Th'harmony of their tongues', their pleasant talk; 'hath into bondage/Brought my diligent ear', made me listen attentively; 'noblest grace she ow'd', her finest virtue; 'put it to the foil', cast it off or made it look bad; 'peerless', without equal; 'features are abroad', how people generally look; 'jewel of my dower' my best virtue; 'precepts', rules.
- Groups to look at, copy and work out the meanings of the following old word forms: 'Alas', 'pray you', 'enjoin'd', "T'will', 'become me', 'beseech', 'glass', 'therein'.

Reading

- Groups to meet after every two episodes to assess the developments of the characters, predict the outcomes of the story and work out the meanings of one of the passages which you have read during the episodes.
- Groups to compare any video version with their experience of *The Tempest* in terms of:
  1. how the story is presented
  2. how the characters are portrayed
  3. what differences there are between their two experiences
  4. how they feel about the two presentations and which they prefer.

Writing

- Children to:
  1. Pretend they are one of: Alonso, Antonio, Miranda, Caliban, Ferdinand, Stephano, Trinculo and Ariel and write the story through the eyes of that character.
  2. Write the story or part of the story for children in Year 4 to read.
  3. Choose a main character and keep a log of his or her developments to the end of the play in terms of personal circumstances, relationships with others and changed attitudes.
  4. Write the main developments in the story in as few words as possible after discussion.
- Children to plan a story about being abandoned on an island to include:
  1. The events that led to their abandonment.
  2. How they felt when they realised where they were.

3. What steps they took to survive.
4. New characters whom they meet.
5. Several happenings which are developed through the following stages: how they start, the build up, the climax or conflict and how it all works out.
- Groups to make new plays out of incidents which are reported by the characters or imaginary incidents:
  1. Prospero and Miranda coming to the island.
  2. The early days with Caliban and how they ended.
  3. Prospero's discovery of Ariel in the pine tree and their early relationship.
  4. Stephano and Trinculo joining the ship.
  5. Alonso and Antonio plotting the overthrow of Prospero.
- Scripts to be developed along the lines suggested in Chapter 3, 'Scripted Plays'.

Dance and drama

- For dance themes look for underlying themes as follows:
  1. drowning and emerging cleansed
  2. changing from worse to better
  3. being trapped, burdened, imprisoned, punished with cramps and stings
  4. aggression being frozen and made harmless.
- Use the various songs and chants as source material for dances. e.g. Ariel's 'Full fathom five thy father lies'.
- Use the characters as source material for shapes and movements. e.g. how might Caliban move when chanting 'Ban-ban c-Caliban has a new master.'
- Groups to make their stories into plays through the following process:
  1. Discuss the possible storylines to be used and what should be included in the play and which characters each child is to enact.
  2. Work out and tell the story.
  3. Improvise it, using their own words and rehearsing it towards a final form.
  4. Scripting the final form, but only after the final performance as a way of recording it.

Music

- Children to:
  1. explore the musical potential of their own bodies: clapping, tapping, clicking, chanting, grunting and singing
  2. experiment with ways of speaking extracts of the text
  3. represent the ideas, sounds and feelings in particular scenes or speeches with a pattern of sounds, e.g. Ariel's account of the sinking of the ship, using musical instruments
  4. set Ariel's songs to music as described in Chapter 3, 'Making Songs'.

Art

● Children to:
1. represent feelings and images in scenes or speeches in colours and shapes to produce abstract paintings: e.g. Caliban's 'Be not afear'd' speech about the beauty of the island.
2. record their impressions of the main characters in a series of drawings at various stages of the play, to be used as a basis for portrait paintings. In these paintings the background should almost be as important as the foreground in communicating the nature of the character. e.g. a portrait of Miranda with images of the dangers she faced as a baby.

● Children to:
1. explore imagery by developing responses in drawings, paintings or sculptures.
2. storyboard a scene or part of a scene to show the main developments in the plot.

References

1. *Encarta 98 Encyclopaedia* (1998) U.S.A.: Microsoft Corporation.
2. Powling, C. (November 1986), 'On the Permanence of Pooh', *Books for Keeps* **41**.
3. Haight, G. S. (1968) *George Eliot, a biography*, 7. London: Oxford University Press.
4. Robinson, E. and Summerfield, G. (eds) (1966) *Selected Poems and Prose of John Clare*, 100. London: Oxford University Press.
5. Bronte, C. (1966) *Jane Eyre*, 53. Harmondsworth: Penguin Books.
6. Bronte (1966) 53.
7. Swift, J. (1967) *Gulliver's Travels*. Harmondsworth: Penguin Books.
8. Cox, C. B. (1989) *English for Ages 5 to 16*. London: Her Majesty's Stationery Office.
9. Austen, J. (1995) *Sense and Sensibility*. Harmondsworth: Penguin Books.
10. Andersen, H. (1966) 'The Princess and the Pea', in *The Snow Queen and Other Tales*. New York: Signet Classics.
11. Iversen, P. S. (1966) 'Introduction', in *The Snow Queen and Other Tales*, X. New York: Signet Classics.
12. Milne, A. A. (1928) *The House at Pooh Corner*, 89–105. London: Methuen Publications.
13. Wilde, O. (1962) 'The Selfish Giant', in *The Happy Prince and Other Stories*. Harmondsworth: Puffin Books.
14. Baum, L. F. (1982) *The Wizard of Oz*. Harmondsworth: Puffin.
15. Burnett, F. H. (1994) *The Secret Garden*. London: Hodder & Stoughton.
16. Longfellow, H. W. (1960) *The Song of Hiawatha*. London: Dent and Dutton.
17. Feest, C. F. (1992) *Native Arts of North America*. London: Thames and Hudson.
18. These can be made simply out of plain fabrics, available cheaply in markets. The basic design is a rectangle of fabric with a hole in the middle for the head and either side for the arms. Sleeves and hems can be added for better finish. Fabric paints should then be used for painting designs on them.
19. Shakespeare, W. (1964) *The Tempest*. London: Methuen Publications.
20. Carter, D. (1998) *Teaching Poetry in the Primary School*. London: David Fulton Publishers.
21. Garfield, L. (1985) *Shakespeare's Stories*. London: Victor Gollancz.

Chapter Six

Using modern children's fiction

Children's literature

The current interest in children's literacy makes it valuable to consider the visibility of books in the lives of most children and the seriousness with which this has been treated by the literary establishment. For instance, although public libraries do not enjoy the central status which they used to have, they have become much more child centred over the last 20 years or so. Most libraries now have a large area designated for children, with inviting places for browsing, often with cushions to lounge on. They may have displays of children's work based on books, regular visits from children's authors and a librarian who specialises in books for children.

In many schools this ethos is continued. No longer is the class collection of books dominated by the dog-eared hardback, printed before the war, about the exploits of an upper class hero. Paperbacks abound, with colourful covers, some in sets for the literacy hour. The titles reflect an eclecticism of taste, which has been spread outwards from libraries, local education authorities and, ultimately, from 'experts' in the field of children's literature. Despite the rigours of the literacy hour, children inhabit a more enlightened book environment than those of previous generations did. There is less 'barking at print' and more reading for meaning, less 'third degree' questioning and more discussion. Here, too, there is every chance that an actual author will visit the school, doing workshops, reading from her work and signing copies of the latest book. This author will no doubt be supported by the regional arts association as well as the school itself.

The child may also have a growing collection of books at home. Many of these will probably be on the bedroom shelf because of an enthusiasm generated by a serial on television such as Goosebumps or The Demon Headmaster or because of a film at the cinema or the subsequent video. Roald Dahl is likely to be there in numbers, with his iconoclastic humour, and the number of authors represented there will be expanding. Consequently, sales of books are greater now than ever before, helped by the rise of the inexpensive paperback. Books, along with CDs and videos, are cool presents to buy for most children at the turn of the millennium.

The picture I am painting is justifiably optimistic and is having a positive impact on the rise of literacy among our children. It will continue to do so as long as the formality brought by the literacy hour doesn't stifle interest. This encouraging picture has been fashioned over many years, with many battles lost and won. A great deal is owed to the much-maligned 1960s, when the golden age of the picture book began, and to the so-called 'real books' movement, so vehemently attacked by politicians who didn't realise that 'real books' actually meant books of literary and artistic quality.

It is strange to imagine that the concept of 'children's literature' is a relatively new one. As an academic subject, studied in the education departments at colleges and universities, it is not much more than 30 years old, yet it is well established now. As Watkins and Sutherland observe: 'In 1992, the Children's Literature Association issued a *Directory of Graduate Studies in Children's Literature* which listed courses at over 200 institutions.'[1]

Children's literature has its own journals, such as the pioneering *Children's Literature in Education*[2], *Signal Magazine*[3], *Books for Keeps*[4] and, in the United States, *The Lion and the Unicorn*[5]. Articles and books of criticism have proliferated in the last 20 years or so and literary critics are beginning to bring to children's literature the 'full range of literary theory'.[6]

Yet the concept of 'children's literature' and even the concept of 'childhood' are relatively new and it was only when the idea of childhood gained ground in the seventeenth century that books could be produced to supply the newly recognised needs of children, as John Rowe Townsend argues: 'Before there could be children's books, there had to be children – children, that is, who were accepted as beings with their own particular needs and interests, not only as miniature men and women.'[7]

It took another 200 years or so for the mass publication of books for children. Yet, even by the start of the First World War, reading was still mainly an activity of the middle and upper classes, illiteracy being rife among working class children. The increase in levels of literacy during the following eighty years created a huge market for children's books, which the educational establishment has encouraged.

Most histories of children's literature date its beginnings to the work of Charles Perrault, the French collector of fairy tales in the late seventeenth century and, in Britain, to John Newbery, who began publishing books for children about 70 years later. This makes children's literature a relatively new branch of the subject with roots in oral tradition and adult literature. To some extent it is considered inferior by critics and even by authors themselves. Universities rarely include children's literature in mainstream English studies and many authors have seen it as a way of increasing their earnings rather than satisfying their creative goals.

Part of the reason for children's literature's relatively low status in the eyes of the literary establishment is that it is seen as a vehicle for educating children. Zohar Shavit argues its development has not been according to 'literary norms' so much as 'social legitimations and motivations' and that this has 'fixed the educational system as a major frame of reference for children's literature'.[8] This view was supported by one of our finest children's authors, Jill Paton Walsh, when she complained that: 'Many teachers see the children's writer, like the children's doctor, the children's psychiatrist, the children's teacher, the children's home, as part of the apparatus of society for dealing with and helping children . . .'[9]

There is also the problem that judgments about quality and suitability are usually made by adults and not by children. How many children's literature prizes have been awarded by panels of children and how many of the winning entries are popular with children? This problem is succinctly summarised by Shavit:

> The children's writer is perhaps the only one who is asked to address one particular audience and at the same time to appeal to another. Society expects the children's writer to be appreciated by both adults ... and children. Yet this demand is both complex and even contradictory by nature because of the different and incompatible tastes of children and adults. But one thing is clear: in order for a children's book to be accepted by adults, it is not enough for it to be accepted by children.[10]

Those of us who have made our careers in primary education are only too aware of this particular problem. We tolerate comics but not Enid Blyton, the most popular children's writer ever in Britain. We used to fear the apparent amorality of Roald Dahl, but have come to accept him because his writing is so good. We seek to edit things out if we can. Even in the literacy lesson plans in this book I have recommended cuts – on the grounds of racism. Whether we are teachers or parents we feel a responsibility for what our children read and watch on television. What is happening is that we are acting as literary critics but with a range of tools more to do with morals and reading skills than literary values and often without fully reading the books ourselves. If we have to continue in this role – and quite clearly there is little alternative – we need to have a set of criteria which is not only about educational but also literary values.

Why teach modern children's fiction?

If children's literature began and developed out of the recognition of children's needs over 300 years ago, it stands to reason that our set of criteria for teaching it should be based there too. We have already seen in Chapter 4 that Bettelheim used fairy tales to treat a very particular set of children's needs, their psychological impairments, and psychological needs must figure highly in any set of criteria for teaching children's literature. Bettelheim's arguments centre on children's subconscious view of themselves, of their relationships with their parents and their need to grow into empowerment. He claimed that, by entering the 'other worlds' of fairy tales, children could play out their fears and learn more about them.

Another key figure from the psychological field is D. W. Harding, whose arguments revolve around his term 'empathic insight'. He sees the reader of a narrative as having two roles. At one and the same time, claims Harding, the reader '. . . fills the dual role of participant and spectator, and as spectator he can when need be turn away from the fantasy events and attend again to the demands of real life.'[11]

The value of this dual activity, according to Harding, is that the spectator can '. . . view ways of life beyond his own range. Contemplating exceptional people, he can achieve an imaginary development of human potentialities that have remained rudimentary in himself or have been truncated after brief growth.'[12]

Now Harding was writing this more than 25 years ago and his emphasis on 'exceptional people' implies a hierarchy with the child at the lower and the character in the literature at the upper end. Although he goes on to claim that as readers of literature we can envisage 'broad types of experience that we know in our own' he stresses a sort of superiority in the experience we witness when reading. He writes of 'a more remarkable way of life' which may bring 'enhanced significance' to the 'ordinary possibilities of our own lives'.[13]

It would be interesting to know the literature Harding had in mind when he developed these ideas. One work he does quote from is Joseph Conrad's *Lord Jim*, which, according to the criteria I set out in Chapter 5, is from 'the classical inheritance'. Perhaps, however, this offers one reason why 'modern' children's literature – in addition to that from the oral and classical traditions – should be taught to children. Although we wish our children to engage with the oral and classical traditions for reasons already developed in this book, we should equally wish for them to meet the literature of their own and recent times.

Harding has in mind 'exceptional people' with 'more remarkable lives' such as Lord Jim, Prospero and Hiawatha, and no teacher or parent would deny children from being onlookers into such fictional lives. However, children also need to be onlookers into lives which are not necessarily any more remarkable than their own. This is one reason for the success of the television serials such as Grange Hill or Byker Grove and for children's addiction to Neighbours, Eastenders and Coronation Street. One of the key developments of modern children's literature is the production of fictions about unexceptional people with unremarkable lives. Often these characters are put in exceptional circumstances and that is where the interest lies. Children can identify in a different way with such characters. They can imagine such children in their class at school. Indeed, many children read about fictional experiences in modern children's literature, which are less remarkable than experiences they have had themselves.

Much of modern children's literature offers children the possibility of being spectators of and participants in lives they can clearly identify with. This is a most important contribution both to children's self knowledge and to their literary development. However, modern children's literature offers more than the possibility of psychological development. The main purposes of this book has been to suggest routes to children's literacy and these cannot be followed entirely with the literature and themes of the past. Children need to read stories not only in the language registers of previous eras but also in those of the present. A classical heritage approach to the teaching of literature to children, used exclusively, would alienate. The language of literature would always appear as problematical, maybe even intimidating. Similarly, an approach based entirely on retellings of stories from the oral tradition might easily make literature a quaint experience, something entirely about the past and about magic. Even written in modern language such fictions would appear remote and having little to do with what the children already know and experience. Such a use of modern language might appear as contrived if it were only used for stories from the past.

Modern children's fiction also offers an increasing range of genres to children, thereby broadening their literary experience. For instance, since the war the historical novel, as written by such authors as Rosemary Sutcliffe and Henry Treece, has made a significant and challenging contribution both to children's knowledge of history and to their literary development. Similar developments have taken place in the science fiction and fantasy novel.

The greatest contribution of modern children's fiction to children's literary and aesthetic developments, however, has been through the widespread use and development of socio-realism. It is in socio-realistic works that children have been able to make those identifications with other children and people who are instantly recognisable figures of modern society. This does not only apply to novels about issues, but also to works of science fiction and fantasy with a socio-realistic context. Even the historical novel has benefited from the rise of socio-realism in children's fiction. So, for instance, the success of Alan Garner's *Elidor*[44] is as much dependent on its socio-realistic context as on its strange other world. Similarly, the power of Robert Westall's Second World War novels derives from his 'modern', realistic treatment of characters and their relationships. A character such as Chas McGill in *The Machine-Gunners*[15] could never have appeared in any book written for children before the 1960s. Socio-realism pervades much of modern children's fiction and, despite any reservations we might have about social issues coming before literary considerations, it has had a positive effect.

Literacy strategy lessons

As far as possible the works of modern children's fiction chosen for the literacy strategy lessons reflect the different genres available. All of them, to a greater or lesser extent, have been affected by the rise of socio-realism, even the fantasy works, Sendak's *Where the Wild Things Are* and Carter's *Misspellboobiland* and the historical novels, Bawden's *Carrie's War* and Magorian's *Goodnight Mister Tom*.

Every work of modern fiction should be introduced in the following way:

- Make large poster versions of the two extracts.
- Read the story, in episodes from Year 2 on, to the children, inviting Reception and Year 1 children to join in with repetitions.
- Establish that they remember each episode by going over the main points.
- Pairs or groups to retell the story to each other with the listeners making corrections.
- Briefly recap the story at the start of each session.
- Groups to recite extracts of the text, rehearsing briefly every day. Give advice on pronouncing each sound correctly.
- Teach children how to change their voices for different characters and for punctuation marks and emphasis. Allow time for experimentation with this.
- When the groups have reached a good level of clarity and expression in speaking their passages they should perform to the whole class.
- Word and sentence level work is based on the two extracts of text provided in each set of notes, however, you might like to use other extracts in addition.
- Work based on every story should conclude with the following kinds of plenary or sharing:
  1. Frequent revision of word work items with regular chanting of the sounds.
  2. Children to practise retelling the story in their own words and reading parts of it, paying due attention to punctuation.
  3. Plays and dances to be rehearsed and performed to audiences, sometimes invited from other classes. Musical pieces to be performed as part of these occasions.
  4. Art to be exhibited in classroom or corridor galleries.
  5. Writing to be anthologised and put on display.

YR: T2. *Maurice Sendak,* **Where the Wild Things Are**[16]

Word and sentence

- Make and label signs with children's pictures for 'Max', 'mother' and 'wild thing'.
- Make and label signs with children's pictures for 'boat', 'bed', and 'room'.
- Arrange 'the', 'his', 'and', 'made', 'of', 'one', 'another', 'said', 'he', 'was', 'to', 'in', 'a', 'with', 'an', 'by', 'for', 'out' and 'are' in alphabetical order on a poster.
- Children to say whenever they recognise a word in the large copy of the story.
- Write and display these phrases: 'his mother called him WILD THING!'; 'he was sent to bed'; 'in Max's room a forest grew and grew – and grew'; 'Max said "BE STILL"'; 'he smelled good things to eat' and 'It was still hot.'
- Children to say when they recognise these phrases in the large version of the story.

Reading

- Discuss the book, asking the children to point to 'cover', 'beginning', 'end', 'a page', 'a line', 'a word', 'a letter' and 'the title'. Say Maurice Sendak wrote the words and painted the pictures and that he is the 'author'.
- When you read from the book, open each page in an exaggerated way and sometimes say, 'This is how you read a book, turning the pages from right to left.'
- Children to repeat this after you.
- Run your finger along the lines, letting your finger dwell on key words and repeat them.
- Children to tell the story in their own words, then ask them if there is any difference between this story and what the book says.
- Children to draw pictures of other things Max might have done when making mischief.
- Groups to discuss:
  1. Why Max gets sent to bed.
  2. What happens to his bedroom.
  3. If it really happened.
  4. Where he goes and how he gets there.
  5. How long it takes him.
  6. What wild things are like.
  7. What Max does to them.
  8. What they do to Max.
  9. What they do together.
  10. How it all ends.

Writing

- Pairs to work out stories about being sent early to bed and to tell them to the class.
- Older children to help to scribe them.

Dance and drama

- Throughout these games use the words from the book as often as possible.
- Work on the line, 'That very night in Max's room a forest grew and grew – and grew'.
- Children to:
    1. make tight shapes, then slowly grow into trees, vines and bushes and into jungle.
    2. recall one of the monsters with 'terrible roars', 'terrible teeth', 'terrible eyes' and 'terrible claws' and try to make it.
    3. improvise – in pairs – a scene in which one is Max making 'mischief of one kind and another' and one Mother calling him 'WILD THING!'
    4. make a 'wild rumpus', ensuring that they do definite wild things with control.
- To stop them say, 'Now stop!' and threaten to send them 'to bed without their supper'.

Music

- Using percussion instruments, children to make sounds for the forest growing in Max's bedroom and a rhythm to accompany the wild rumpus dancing.

Art

- Children to make pictures to go with their own stories.

Y1: T1. Judith Kerr, Mog, the Forgetful Cat[17]

Text

1. The garden always made Mog very excited.
   She smelled all the smells.
   She chased the birds.
   She climbed the trees.
   She ran round and round
   with a big fluffed-up tail.
   And then she forgot the cat flap.
   She forgot that she had a cat flap.
   She wanted to go back into the house,
   but she couldn't remember how.
   In the end she sat outside the kitchen window
   and meowed until someone let her in.

2. Mog ran out of the room
   and right through the house
   and out of her cat flap.
   She was very sad.
   The garden was dark.
   The house was dark too.
   Mog sat in the dark
   and thought dark thoughts.

She thought, 'Nobody likes me.
They've all gone to bed.
There's no one to let me in.
And they haven't even given me my supper.'
Then she noticed something.
The house was not quite dark.
There was a little light moving about.

Word and sentence

1.
- Write 'Mog', 'ran', 'big', 'cat' and 'let' on a flipchart.
- Children to find the words in the passage. Ensure that they say these words *frequently*.
- Children to choose one sentence from the passage (e.g. 'She chased the birds.'), draw a picture for it and write the sentence as a caption underneath.

2.
- Write 'sad', 'sat', 'bed', 'not' and 'was' on the flipchart.
- Children to look for more examples of these basic words and add them to the list.
- Print the passage on a sheet. Children to search it for capital letters and full stops, put a red ring round capital letters and a blue ring round full stops.

Reading

- Reread the story. Children to say what is in the pictures, their descriptions to be word-processed with copies attached underneath the pictures.
- Children to provide anecdotes about pets, particularly about the things they do which might cause their parents to say 'Bother that . . . !'
- Groups to recite a passage of about 12 lines, then tell the story using their own words.
- Discuss the differences.
- Pairs to describe what the garden is like to Mog in the daytime and at night.
- Confident readers to read other 'Mog' books and to talk to the class about them.

Writing

- Children to write their pet anecdotes or to make up a pet story.
- Children to make a simple book for their pet stories as follows:
  1. Draw a short series of pictures of the story on A5 sheets.
  2. Write a sentence or caption underneath each.
  3. Fold an A4 sheet for the cover, draw a picture for it and at the top write the title and at the bottom write 'Written and illustrated by . . .' and their name.
  4. Fix the sheets inside the cover with thin smears of glue along each one.

Dance and drama

- Children to:
  1. Start in rolled-up-cat-asleep positions then perform cat-like stretches, walks and runs, using the pictures in the books for ideas.

2. Mime the incidents in the book as cats.
3. Act out an incident in their own words and movements.
4. Improvise the burglar scene using their own words and movements.
5. Include some of the actual words which the characters use.

Art

● To enhance the quality of the individual storybooks children to practise the drawings, using a variety of tools, including coloured pencils.

Music

● Children to make simple sound effects to accompany their plays.

Y2: T1. Antonia Barber, **The Mousehole Cat**[18]

Text

1. Once there lived in the village a cat whose name was Mowzer.
    She had an old cottage with a window overlooking the harbour, an old rocking-chair with patchwork cushions and an old fisherman called Tom.
    Mowzer had had many kittens in her time but they had all grown up and left home.
    Her eldest son kept the inn on the quayside. It was noisy and smoky and his man had once spilled beer on Mowzer's head as he was drawing a pint.
    So she did not go there very often.
    One of her daughters kept the shop on the corner. It was busy and crowded and her lady once stepped on Mowzer's tail as she was weighing out some vegetables.
    So she did not go there very often either.
    Sometimes Mowzer felt that her children had not trained their people properly.
    Her own pet, Tom, was very well behaved. He never spilled the cream when he was filling her saucer. He always stoked the range to a beautiful golden glow. He rocked the rocking-chair at just the right speed. He knew the exact spot behind her left ear where Mowzer liked to be tickled. What was more, he never wasted his time drawing pints of beer or weighing out vegetables.

2. Then the Great Storm-Cat played with them as a cat plays with a mouse. He would let them loose for a little as they fought their way towards the fishing grounds. Then down would come his giant cat's paw in a flurry of foam and water. But he did not yet strike to sink them, for that would have spoiled his sport.
    When they reached the fishing grounds the sea was so rough that it was hard to put out the nets.
    'I fancy you must sing again, Mowzer, my handsome,' said Tom, 'for your voice seems to soothe the sea like the sirens of old.'
    So Mowzer sang again, longer and louder than she had ever sung before. Indeed, old Tom was forced to block up his ears, so that her siren-song should not distract him from the business of fishing.

And again, the Great Storm-Cat paused in his play and sang with her until the nets were safely shot.

All day they fished in a seething sea. The waves were so high and the clouds so low that they soon lost sight of the shore.

And all the time the Great Storm-Cat played with the little boat, striking it and then loosing it, but never quite sinking it. And whenever his claws grew too sharp, Mowzer would sing to him to soften the edge of his anger.

Word and sentence

1.
- Write *ow*: 'Mowzer', 'crowded'; *ow*: 'own', 'grown', 'glow' on a flipchart.
- Children to find the words in the extract.
- Write *ee* sound as in 'quayside', 'either', 'cream', 'beautiful' and 'speed'. Children to find other examples of these spellings. List on flipchart.
- Using the context, children to work out the meanings of 'harbour', 'range', 'quayside' and 'drawing a pint'.

2.
- Revise 'vowel' and 'consonant'. Children to find and list five consonants and three vowels in any sentence in the extract.
- Write *ed*: 'played', 'spoiled', 'reached', 'forced'. Children to identify the original words these are based on and make a chart: 'play' – 'played', 'spoil' – 'spoiled' and so on.
- Revise use of capital letters: at beginnings of sentences, for names, headings and titles. Children to find the words in the extract with capital letters, list them and say whether they are beginnings of sentence words or names.

Reading

- At '. . . how warm and welcoming the window looked.' children to predict what will happen next to Mowzer and Tom.
- Children to recite their extracts then tell that part of the story in their own words. What differences do they notice?
- Keep the same groups for discussion work and set these questions. What happened when:
  1. The 'terrible winter' came?
  2. Tom and Mowzer left the harbour in the boat?
  3. Mowzer sang her song?
- Continue these discussions with 'What did':
  1. The Great Storm-Cat do when Mowzer purred?
  2. The people of Mousehole do when they noticed Tom's boat missing?
And why did:
  1. Mowzer like Tom?
  2. Tom go out into the storm in his boat?
  3. Mowzer go with Tom into the stormy sea?

Writing

- Children to write:
  1. About the differences between reading and telling the story in their extracts.
  2. Answers to the questions discussed above
- Children to recollect dangerous experiences they have had and make a story with a clear beginning, middle and end, tell it to a partner, then develop it, writing about:
  1. The characters and where they live and what they like to do.
  2. What started the dangerous situation.
  3. What happened to the characters.
  4. How the whole incident ended.

Dance and drama

- Explore the various movements of the sea and build into a dance. Children to:
  1. Make small wave shapes, gently allowing them to break and reform and making swishing sounds with their mouths.
  2. Increase the size and intensity of the waves breaking and the volume of the swishing.
  3. Join into twos, threes, then fours and so on to increase the sea movements and sounds.
  4. Try to make their waves have a cat feature, perhaps claw-shaped fingers or teeth bared.
- Make the Great Storm-Cat by gathering the class to make a great wave shape that rises, breaks, falls and rises again, howling and meowing loudly.

Music

- Children work on the sounds of cats and the sea as follows:
  1. Imitate the sounds that cats make.
  2. Imitate the sounds the sea makes.
  3. Make a pattern of sounds with their voices which follows the sea from gently breaking to the Great Storm-Cat, adding cat sounds until the two merge in a crescendo.
- Add the voice of Mowzer singing and purring and calming it down. Children to:
  1. Make a sweeter set of cat noises – meowings and purrings, not hissings and growling.
  2. Add this at the crescendo, causing the Great Storm-Cat to quieten down.

Art

- Children to:
  1. Work out alternative ways of representing the Great Storm-Cat, trying to show a storm at sea that has a cat look about it.
  2. Doodle with a soft pencil to try to find ideas that will work as paintings for this.
  3. Work out how it will be painted.
  4. Draw the basic lines in chalk onto a large sheet of drawing paper.

5. Mix their own colours.
6. Paint the Great Storm-Cat paintings, experimenting with the shapes they can make in paint with the brush.

● Produce illustrations for the class anthology of personal stories.

Y3: T1. *Roald Dahl,* Danny, the Champion of the World[19]

Text

1. I must pause here to tell you something about Mr. Victor Hazell. He was a brewer of beer and he owned a large brewery. He was rich beyond words, and his property stretched for miles along either side of the valley. All the land around us belonged to him, everything on both sides of the road, everything except the small patch of ground on which our filling-station stood. That patch belonged to my father. It was a little island in the middle of the vast ocean of Mr. Hazell's estate.

   Mr. Victor Hazell was a roaring snob and he tried desperately to get in with what he believed were the right kind of people. He hunted with the hounds and gave shooting parties and wore fancy waistcoats. Every week-day he drove his enormous silver Rolls-Royce past our filling-station on his way to the brewery. As he flashed by we would sometimes catch a glimpse of his great glistening beery face above the wheel, pink as a ham, all soft and inflamed with drinking too much beer.

   'No,' my father said, 'I do not like Mr. Victor Hazell one little bit. I haven't forgotten the way he spoke to you last year when he came in for a fill-up.'

   I hadn't forgotten it either. Mr. Hazell had pulled up alongside the pumps in his glistening gleaming Rolls-Royce and had said to me, 'Fill her up and look sharp about it.' I was eight years old at the time. He didn't get out of the car, he just handed me the key to the cap of the petrol tank and as he did so, he barked out, 'And keep your filthy little hands to yourself, d'you understand?' (pages 52 to 53)

2. 'That's the head keeper,' my father said. 'His name is Rabbetts.'

   'Do we have to go home, Dad?'

   'Home!' my father cried. 'My dear boy, we're just beginning! Come in here.'

   There was a gate on our right leading into a field, and we climbed over it and sat down behind the hedge.

   'Mr. Rabbetts is also due for his supper,' my father said. 'You mustn't worry about him.'

   We sat quietly behind the hedge waiting for the keeper to walk past us on the way home. A few stars were showing, and a bright three-quarter moon was coming up over the hills behind us in the east.

   'We have to be careful of that dog,' my father said. 'When they come by, hold your breath and don't move a muscle.'

   'Won't the dog smell us anyway?' I asked.

   'No,' my father said. 'There's no wind to carry the scent. Look out! Here they come! Don't move!'

   The keeper came loping softly down the track with the dog padding quick and soft-footed at his heel. I took a deep breath and held it as they went by.

When they were at some distance away, my father stood up and said, 'It's all clear. He won't be coming back tonight.'

'Are you sure?'

'I'm positive, Danny.'

'What about the other one, the one in the clearing?'

'He'll be gone too.'

'Mightn't one of them be waiting for us at the bottom of the track?' I asked. 'By the gap in the hedge?'

'There wouldn't be any point in him doing that,' my father said. 'There's at least twenty different ways of reaching the road when you come out of Hazell's Wood. Mr. Rabbetts knows that.'

We stayed behind the hedge for a few minutes more just to be on the safe side.

Word and sentence

1.
- By using context clues, children to work out then check the meanings of the following words: 'brewery', 'property', 'belonged', 'vast', 'glistening' and 'inflamed'.
- Children to list words with three syllables.
- Children to write *tch*: 'stretched', 'patch', 'catch'
- Children to work out how else can the *tch* sound can be spelt: ('much').

2.
- Children to find more three-syllable words and add to chart.
- Children to find and write these verbs: 'climbed', 'sat', 'padding', 'waiting' and 'stayed', adding the name or names of the characters who perform these actions.
- Children to revise speech marks, exclamation marks and question marks.
- Groups to look for them in the extract, working out which characters speak, who uses exclamation marks and who asks most of the questions.

Reading

- After Chapter 8, children to compare the opening paragraph of Chapter 8 (page 73), with the final paragraph of Chapter 1 (page 15), saying which words, phrases and sentences create the two different feelings.
- Early in the project groups to discuss:
  1. the filling-station in the story compared with filling-stations these days
  2. stories they have been told at home
  3. importance of going to school
  4. favourite pastimes
  5. poaching pheasants – right or wrong?
- At the end of Chapter 16, groups to recite three pages of the book to be turned into a playscript as follows:
  1. Read the passage aloud, taking turns and trying to show changes of voices.
  2. Decide who will speak the characters' words and who read the story.

Writing

- Children to:
  1. Develop their spoken arguments into writing.
  2. Write about one of the following: Danny, Danny's father, Mr. Victor Hazell, Doc Spencer or Captain Lancaster.
  3. Describe their favourite incidents and say why they like them.
  4. Add a short incident to the story with plenty of dialogue, using the correct conventions.
  5. Make their three pages into playscripts following the guidelines in Chapter 3, 'Scripted Plays'.
- Children to plan and write their own stories, based on incidents and themes in the book as follows: a classroom in the olden days; almost being caught; working out a trick; a crazy adventure; meeting a frightening grown up; choice of their own.

Drama and music

- Children to:
  1. add sound effects and composed music to the plays for voices, composing the music using percussion instruments and keyboards.
  2. improvise their own scenes based on their stories.

Art

- Children to paint the various settings, using the descriptions of them: e.g. Hazell's woods from the inside and the outside.
- Extend this by showing the children pictures of woods painted by artists of the past.
- Children to:
  1. paint portraits of the characters differently from the illustrator, Quentin Blake, using initial descriptions.
  2. illustrate their own stories, using a simple cartoon style like Quentin Blake.

Y4: T2. Dennis Carter, Misspellboobiland[20]

Text

1. Jay started running into the sea. Penny leapt after him. They splashed huge curves of water, silver water shattering like broken glass, followed by khaki sand and pebble-filled water. From the hotel they appeared as stage one of the invasion force with their haze of water until they sank with exhaustion under it. Hopefully drowned according to some no doubt. But they did eventually emerge from the sea to collapse onto their air-beds, gasping and laughing.

   On the strength of their becoming friends again because of the fight, Penny got two ice-creams and, as they licked them, they began to enjoy their holiday at last. Jay moved his air-bed nearer to Penny's and they started doing something they often did when bored. They made up rude stories about the family who were sunbathing next to their parents.

   Jay said, 'Have you seen their dad with his beer belly?'

Penny answered, 'Yeah. It's so big it's . . . it's his hump. Like a camel's, you know, but on the front.'

Relishing this comparison, Jay added, 'Every so often notice a little tremble running up and down him. That tremble begins in his belly . . .'

'. . . and goes straight to his throat,' said Penny. 'But tell me maestro,' she continued, 'what could be the cause of this amazing wobble? Surely it is camel-man drinking in a little water . . . I mean beer, from his hump.'

'And their mum's wobbly bum goes well with the tremble coming from their dad's tum. In fact, it makes her hippomum,' Jay said with great emphasis.

'Camel-tum-dad,' Penny went on.

'And hippo-bum-mum,' Penny echoed.

'What a terrifically trembly couple,' they sang out in unison. Then they started looking for other 'beasts' to make up rude stories and songs about. But before they could they both dropped off to sleep. (pages 5 to 6)

2. As they journeyed, grey of dawn melted to blue and rags of darkness were washed by light. Fresh winds blew them on their quest. They were solemn and quiet, as if aware of the enormity of their task and the dangers that awaited them. Brut swayed in a steady, walking rhythm. Figling flapped and glided, flapped and glided just above them and the silver birds flew in a V-formation much higher so that they could see all that was happening or about to happen.

Gradually, they rose onto a magnificent plateau, where the air was so sweet it refreshed the spirits like the finest drink. Jay thought it must be like being in the lands of the great gods of mythology he was always reading about. He imagined meeting Zeus or Woden.

'This,' he thought, 'might be the place where Thor made his hammer. Or this whole island might be the one visited by Odysseus during his twenty-year voyage from the wars of Troy. One of these rocky places might be the home of Polyphemus, the one-eyed giant, who liked eating Odysseus's men.'

Jay's daydreams were interrupted by Brut, who stopped, raised a front foot and pointed towards the thin points of rock in the north, 'Those mountains and all that dismal land around them are Turnig territory. Those are the highest mountains on the island and the rocks are sharper and rougher to cross than any others. The Turnigs live in holes and caverns amongst them. When they attack they come at you from all directions, so many different directions you wouldn't know where to expect them next. But, don't worry, you two. We'll get past them.'

Word and sentence

1.
- Write *bb*: 'wobble'; *cc*: 'according'; *ll*: 'following', 'hopefully', 'collapse', 'eventually', 'belly'; *nn*: 'Penny', 'running'; *pp*: 'dropped'; *rr*: 'terrifically'; *tt*: 'shattering', 'little' on chart.
- Break 'invasion' into its component syllables: *in – va – sion.*
- Children to:

1. practise speaking and spelling each syllable and the whole word;
2. repeat this with the words: 'exhaustion', 'according', 'becoming', 'something', 'sunbathing', 'comparison'.

● Write adverbs ending in *ly*: 'Hopefully', 'eventually' and 'terrifically'. Children to locate their roots: 'hopeful', 'eventual' and 'terrific' and discuss differences.

2.

● Revise adjectives.
● Children to:
   1. find the adjectives which describe the following nouns: 'winds', 'birds', 'air', 'drink', 'foot', 'land' and 'rocks'.
   2. work out alternative adjectives and say how these would change the meaning of the extract.
   3. consider the use of figurative language in the first paragraph and the impression 'grey of dawn melted to blue', 'rags of darkness were washed by light' and 'Fresh winds blew them'.

Reading

● Discuss imaginary worlds and how they think the 'Misspellboobiland' author invented these two kingdoms.
● After they have worked out their own ideas tell the children the process went like this:
   1. Dennis Carter, when teaching Year 3 children, was amused by some of the strange spelling mistakes made by members of his class. He started to invent imaginary creatures for them. The first one was 'Brut', a misspelling of 'brought'!
   2. After writing the song lyrics for these characters, he started to imagine where they all might live.
   3. Then he wondered why they would be like they are and what would happen if two children discovered them.
   4. The lyrics became songs that the creatures sang to introduce themselves.
   5. He started to write the story, but it took years of revisions to get into the final form.
● Groups to read through Chapter 3, looking for examples of details in the descriptions of the island which create the impression of an unusual place.
● At the end of Chapter 6 children to find descriptions which make you expect that something dramatic or tense is about to happen.
● Continue to collect examples of detailed descriptions which 1) create unusual impressions of places and 2) prepare you for a dramatic incident.
● Groups to recall and list other stories about imaginary worlds. In what ways are they similar and in what ways different from 'Misspellboobiland'?

Writing

● Children to:
   1. create an imaginary world of their own during a brainstorming session and write a paragraph which describes this place, using descriptions and figurative language.

2. imagine something dramatic happening in their imaginary worlds and write a paragraph which will lead into that incident, using descriptions and figurative language.

- Children then to close eyes and imagine their made up world, then to imagine they are going there with a friend, how they get there and what they find there.
- Children to tell the story outline to a friend and invite responses and tell it again.
- Children to write the story, remembering to make their settings with good use of description and to build up to their dramatic scenes with good use of detailed description.

Dance and drama

- Explore the theme of monsters and beasts through making shapes and moving according to them. Children to:
  1. look for 'monstrous' or 'beastly' descriptions for the dance and drama ideas
  2. shape a partner to match the descriptions
  3. refine the monsters according to facial expression, position of hands and arms, position of legs and trunk, position of chest and head
  4. try out the monster and see if it matches the description in the text
  5. make new monsters, following the same process
  6. work out short improvised scenes in which one is the monster, the other someone lost in the imaginary world of the monster.
- Groups to 'share' monsters, improvise meeting scenes, then work out short plays with more than one scene.
- As part of the music work, children also to work out a dance to accompany the songs of each of the Misspellboobi creatures.

Music

- After Chapter 10, groups to make a song out of one of the Misspellboobi lyrics, following the suggestions in Chapter 3, 'Art and Music'.
- Work out an arrangement on percussion and tuned instruments to accompany the song and dance.

Art

- Children to:
  1. represent descriptions of settings in pencil in sketchbooks and develop into paintings
  2. respond to descriptions of characters in the story in sketchbooks, before painting them
  3. develop further through paintings of settings and creatures from the children's own stories and ideas in movement and drama lessons.

Y5: T1. Jan Needle, My Mate Shofiq[21]

Text

1. The Pakistani kids were just coming into good brick-bunging range, and he'd seen Whitehead's lot getting up a nice pile of good-sized rocks to fling, when Bernard caught a movement out of the corner of his eye, away over to his right. He looked round, risking missing the first shot of the war, to see if he could pick it out.

   Over that way it was a right jumble of old, half-down houses, the beginnings of a new estate, and the ruins of another mill, the Muscovy, that still had some bits of old wrecked weaving machines in it. Bernard stared, into the wind, with his eyes watering badly. He'd almost given up, decided he'd been mistaken, when he saw it again. There was someone, someone hiding among the remains of the third terrace along, and creeping towards him.

   He flicked his eyes from the shape, to the victims, to the Whiteheads. He squeezed his frozen finger-ends into his eyes to get the tears out, to get a clearer view. One of the little kids out front began to giggle at something, high and squeaky. Pat Broome weighed up a stone in her hand; she'd soon put a stop to that!

   The figure along the way moved from an old lav, full into Bernard's view. He knew him! He was in the same class! It was a bloke called Shofiq, or something. Shofiq Rahman or something. The two little girls who'd looked familiar clicked. They were his sisters, all dressed up in silk pyjamas while Shofiq wore jeans and a jumper. Blimey – even in this weather he never had a coat on, just jeans and a jumper.

   Bernard watched with extra interest, because he knew Shofiq. Not to talk to, of course, because he didn't talk much in class, when Miss told him to. He was very quiet, and very dark brown, and he had a funny smell to him, like an Indian restaurant, like all the Pakis. But he'd thumped some lad once, not so long ago, and none of the kids who like to bash up the blackies ever touched him. He couldn't take on Bobby Whitehead though, that was obvious. Bobby Whitehead was the champ, he was an ace fighter.

2. The only other confrontation, when Bernard had got them all together to tell them Shofiq was 'in', was over the word Paki. Even Bernard hadn't realized that Shofiq hated it – he'd even addressed his first note to 'The Paki' he recalled with a blush – and at first he'd been inclined to laugh at it. But Shofiq was serious.

   'I can't rightly explain,' he said, 'but it's horrible. I mean I don't call you lot Whities, or something . . . it sounds . . .'

   'Ah rubbish, lad,' said Terry. 'Everyone calls Pakis Pakis. It stands to reason. I mean, my dad calls Pakis Pakis; and blackies. Like West Indian kids gets called Niggers and Chinese is Chinkies. I mean, it's just what you get called, it don't mean nowt.'

   'It does, it does!' said Shofiq. 'I'll tell you, it means . . .'

   He was helpless. He couldn't explain.

   'I just wish you wouldn't, that's all,' he ended lamely.

   'Rubbish!' said Terry firmly. 'I'll call you what I like, and you're a Paki, so there.'

   Shofiq started to push up his sleeves.

'All right then, Smelly White Pig,' he said grimly. 'Take your coat off, lad, 'cause I'm going to batter you.'

Maureen solved it in the end by pointing out that no one was allowed to call Bernard Bernie. Bern was all right, or even Slobberchops. But not Bernie. They discussed as to why, but he couldn't rightly say. But he hated it, and that was that. Terry, who wasn't thick, agreed that he'd not call Shofiq a Paki.

'It's not just me, though,' said Shofiq. 'Everybody hates it, it's rotten. But thanks, Terry.'

'Well I won't call any of 'em – you – Pakis in future,' said Maureen. 'Pakistanis is good enough for me.'

Shofiq giggled: 'Or Indians, or Bangladeshis, or Bengalis, eh? How about British? It's on me birth certificate!' (Pages 11 to 12)

Introduction

Jan Needle's novel *My Mate Shofiq* sensitively examines the problems encountered by the Pakistani community in a Lancashire mill town in the 1970s. Although many things have changed in British society since those days, the problems caused by racial bigotry are still very much with us. In the novel we witness the classic characteristics of racism in action, from casual prejudice against a minority culture's clothing, habits, food, language and religious practices to outright discrimination and violence. The novel provides an honest and powerful focus on a social problem which stubbornly refuses to go away.

Word and sentence

1.
- Using the context, children to work out then check the meaning of: 'brick-bunging', 'fling', 'the first shot of the war'; 'right jumble', 'estate', 'mill', 'wrecked weaving machines' 'terrace' and 'clicked'. List with the children's guesses on the flipchart.
- Discuss racial prejudice, inviting anecdotes. Say that racism often shows itself in the words we use. Children to look for evidence of racist attitudes in the language used ('funny smell', 'Pakis' and 'blackies').
- Discuss verbs. Tell them that the verbs tell us which characters are making things happen.
- Groups to track one of Bernard, the 'Pakistani kids', 'the Whiteheads' and Shofiq:
  1. Discuss then write down what their characters are doing: e.g. 'Bernard is watching'; 'Shofiq is creeping up to defend the Pakistani kids'.
  2. List the verbs which apply to the characters: e.g. Bernard – 'caught', 'looked', 'watched'.
  3. Write what impression this gives: e.g. Bernard – 'watching' creates the impression of someone who is still.

2.
- Groups to discuss the argument between Shofiq and Terry. Why is the word 'Paki' offensive? Establish that it is prejudiced people who, for many years, have called Pakistani's 'Paki' with contempt, that has made the word itself abusive.
- Pairs to look at the layout of the dialogue, draw up and write rules about how this is

done: e.g. a new speech starts on a new paragraph; speech marks are closed after a full stop or comma. Discuss as a class.

- Pairs to turn one piece of direct speech into reported speech: e.g. 'I can't rightly explain,' he said, 'but it's horrible.' becomes 'He said that he couldn't rightly explain but that it is horrible.' Discuss which is better and why.

Reading

- Children to establish logs for each of the main characters or groups of characters and regularly to make notes on:
  1. Words spoken. Positive or negative or neither?
  2. Deeds. What exactly did the character do? Positive or negative?
  3. Description. How was the character described? Positive or negative?
  4. Do you like, dislike, feel sorry for or have other feelings for the character?
  5. Relationships. Did the character get on well, badly or neither with others?
- Groups to investigate racism in newspapers and television for incidents of racial problems, record and discuss:
  1. the sort of incidents reported
  2. the number involving violence
  3. the action taken by the police or other authorities.
- Groups to discuss similarities and differences between the Pakistani and the White communities.

Writing

- Using their logs children to write an evaluation of one character or a group of characters.
- After Chapter 15, groups to turn a chapter into a playscript, following the suggestions in Chapter 3, 'Making Playscripts'.

Dance and drama

- Children to:
  1. Rehearse and record their plays for sharing with an audience.
  2. Make tableaux vivants (as in Chapter 3) for showing the essence of vital incidents: e.g. in pages 72 to 73 Bernard looks through Shofiq's window and witnesses a scene of high tension: three males and two females, one male dominant, a mother sitting and being hugged by her daughter standing.

Art

- Children to:
  1. Use descriptions of the characters as a basis for drawings in sketchbooks, then work one drawing into a larger scale portrait in a medium of their choice. If necessary, research Pakistani dress.
  2. Use the tableaux vivants as a basis for developing illustrations of key scenes, with the actors holding their positions while the artists do their sketchbook drawings, which can be developed later into fuller works.

Y6: T3. Nina Bawden, Carrie's War[22]

Compared with Michelle Magorian, *Goodnight Mister Tom*[23]

Text

1. Carrie had often dreamed about coming back. In her dreams she was twelve years old again; short, scratched legs in red socks and scuffed, brown sandals, walking along the narrow, dirt path at the side of the railway line to where it plunged down, off the high ridge, through the Druid's Grove. The yew trees in the Grove were dark green and so old that they had grown twisted and lumpy, like arthritic fingers. And in Carrie's dream, the fingers reached out for her, plucking at her hair and her skirt as she ran. She was always running by the end of this dream, running away from the house, uphill towards the railway line.

   But when she did come back, with her own children, the railway line had been closed. The sleepers had been taken up and the flat, stony top of the ridge was so overgrown with blackberries and wild rose and hazelnut bushes that it was like pushing through a forgotten forest in a fairy tale. The tangled wood round Sleeping Beauty's castle. Pulling off the sticky brambles that clung to their jeans, Carrie's children said, 'No one's been here for hundreds of years . . .'

   'Not hundreds, *thousands* . . .'

   'A hundred, thousand years. A million, billion, trillion . . .'

   'Only about thirty,' Carrie said. She spoke as if this was no time at all. 'I was here, with Uncle Nick, thirty years ago. During the war – when England was at war with Germany. The Government sent the children out of the cities so they shouldn't be bombed. We weren't told where we were going. Just told to turn up at our schools with a packed lunch and a change of clothes, then we went to the station with our teachers. There were whole train loads of children sent away like that . . .' ('Carrie's War', pages 7 to 8)

2. 'Yes,' said Tom bluntly, on opening the front door. 'What d'you want?'

   A harassed middle-aged woman in a green coat and felt hat stood on his step. He glanced at the armband on her sleeve. She gave him an awkward smile.

   'I'm the Billeting Officer for this area,' she began.

   'Oh yes, and what's that got to do wi' me?'

   She flushed slightly. 'Well, Mr, Mr . . .'

   'Oakley. Thomas Oakley.'

   'Ah, thank you, Mr Oakley.' She paused and took a deep breath. 'Mr Oakley, with the declaration of war imminent . . .'

   Tom waved his hand. 'I knows all that. Git to the point. What d'you want?' He noticed a small boy at her side.

   'It's him I've come about,' she said. 'I'm on my way to your village hall with the others.'

   'What others?'

   She stepped to one side. Behind the large iron gate which stood at the end of the graveyard were a small group of children. Many of them were filthy and very poorly clad. Only a handful had a blazer or a coat. They all looked bewildered and exhausted. One tiny dark-haired girl in the front was hanging firmly on to a new teddy-bear.

The woman touched the boy at her side and pushed him forward.

'There's no need to tell me,' said Tom. 'It's obligatory and it's for the war effort.'

'You are entitled to choose your child, I know,' began the woman apologetically.

Tom gave a snort.

'But,' she continued, 'his mother wants him to be with someone who's religious or near a church. She was quite adamant. Said she would only let him be evacuated if he was.'

Tom took a second look at the child. The boy was thin and sickly-looking, pale with limp sandy hair and dull grey eyes.

'His name's Willie,' said the woman.

Willie, who had been staring at the ground, looked up. Round his neck, hanging from a piece of string, was a cardboard label. It read 'William Beech'.

Tom was well into his sixties, a healthy, robust, stockily-built man with a head of thick white hair. Although he was of average height, in Willie's eyes he was a towering giant with skin like coarse, wrinkled brown paper and a voice like thunder.

He glared at Willie. 'You'd best come in,' he said abruptly.

Introduction

- *Carrie's War* (CW) will be considered as the main novel for teachers to read to their classes. *Goodnight Mister Tom* (GMT) will be considered more as a secondary text for the children to read in groups and this will require a set of copies.
- Read CW without any cuts, but as GMT is stronger when dealing with William Beech's problems in London and his growing relationship with Tom Oakley cut Chapters 19 to 23.

Word, sentence and text

Comparing the extracts

- The two extracts of text are the opening paragraphs of each book. Children to:
  1. Decide from whose point of view the books are written and collect evidence.
  2. Show how the authors take the reader into the story and how effective they are.
  3. Compare the length of sentences and explain why they are longer in one than the other.
  4. Compare the amount of direct speech in each, how often each character speaks and discuss the effect of this on arousing interest.
  5. Investigate what is learnt about evacuation, listing the facts they learn from each extract.
  6. Discuss the overall impression each creates.
  7. Make notes for written pieces.

Carrie's War

- Children to keep a character log about one of Carrie, Nick, Mr Evans, Auntie Lou, Johnny Gotobed, Hepzibah Green and Albert Sandwich, with entries made after each episode in which the character appears, as follows:
  1. What did the character do?
  2. How did the character get on with other characters?
  3. Did the character show any new attitudes or behaviour?
- After Chapter 10, children to write character studies, using their logs.
- Groups to list what new facts about the war have been discovered after every episode.
- After Chapter 7, children to prepare their own notes, share them in discussion then write a comparison between Mr Evans's grocery shop and Druid's Bottom as follows:
  1. Describe the shop and the streets and town around it.
  2. Describe Druid's Bottom and the countryside around it.
  3. Compare life in the grocery shop with life in Druid's Bottom.
  4. Where would you prefer to be billeted and why?
- Children to:
  1. Keep journals in which they summarise the most important incidents in the story and record their own feelings about them.
  2. At the end of the story write a brief synopsis and review of the book for a particular child in a different class.

Goodnight Mister Tom

- Children to keep character logs about one of the following: Tom, Willie, Willie's mother, Zach and Lucy with entries made after each episode in which the character appears, as above.
- Groups to list what new facts about the war have been discovered after every episode.
- Children to:
  1. Make notes (after Chapter 18) and write a comparison between Little Weirwold and Willie's home and streets in London.
  2. Keep a journal to summarise the important incidents and their feelings about them.
  3. At the end of the story write a brief synopsis and a review of the book for a particular child in a different class.

Comparisons between Carrie's War *and* Goodnight Mister Tom

- Using character logs, groups to compare:
  1. Nick and Willie.
  2. Mr Evans and Tom.
  3. Albert Sandwich and Zach.

- Groups to discuss:
    1. with examples, which novel provides more information about the war;
    2. which author is more effective in describing the settings for her scenes;
    3. which are the three most important incidents in each novel?
- Children to write a comparison between the books regarding the authors' success in keeping their interest, descriptions of characters and settings and the strengths and weaknesses of each.

Story-writing

- Children to find a person who was a child during the war, then:
    1. ask the person to tell the story about being a child during the war
    2. remember the story
    3. confirm the details of the story with the person
    4. retell it to a friend and to their families
    5. map out which incidents will be in the written version of the story and in what order
    6. decide what the characters and settings will be
    7. write intensively in first draft, without dictionaries or thesauruses
    8. review each chapter with a critical eye and with the dictionary and thesaurus
    9. ask a friend to read the story and provide constructive criticism
    10. write a final version.

Dance, drama and music

- Groups to discuss the making of a play about life on the home front during the Second World War, bearing in mind:
    1. the use of material from the novels, from history books, video footage or photographs
    2. the use of plots from one of the stories they are writing
    3. using the teacher only for advice when they need it
    4. the use of movement sequences
    5. the use of composed or recorded music from the period to create atmosphere.

Art

- Children to:
    1. find an evocative description of a place in either of the novels and to develop it into a picture, using any medium, including three dimensional materials: e.g. a model of the inside of Mr Evans's grocery store.
    2. make a series of black and white illustrations for their extended stories as in the novels

References

1. Watkins, T. and Sutherland, Z. (1995) 'Contemporary Children's Literature (1970-present)' in Hunt, P. (ed.) *Children's Literature, an illustrated history*. London: Oxford University Press.
2. Fox, G. (ed.), *Children's Literature in Education*. New York: Human Sciences Press.
3. Chambers, A. and Chambers, N. (eds), *Signal Magazine*. Stroud: Signal Publications.
4. Powling, C. (ed.), *Books for Keeps*. London: The Bodley Head.

5. *The Lion and the Unicorn*. United States: Johns Hopkins University Press.

6. Watkins and Sutherland (1995) 290.

7. Townsend, J. R. (1977) *Written for Children*. Harmondsworth: Penguin.

8. Shavit, Z. (1986) *Poetics of Children's Literature*, 35. Athens, Georgia: University of Georgia Press.

9. Walsh, J. P. (1973) 'The Writer's Responsibility', in *Children's Literature in Education* 4: 30–36. New York: Human Sciences Press.

10. Shavit (1986) 37.

11. Harding, D. W. (1977) 'Psychological processes in the reading of fiction' in Meek, M. (ed.) *The Cool Web*, 62. London: Bodley Head.

12. Harding, (1977) 70.

13. Harding, (1977) 70.

14. Garner, A. (1965) *Elidor*. London: Collins.

15. Westall, R. (1975) *The Machine-Gunners*. London: Macmillan Publishers.

16. Sendak, M. (1967) *Where the Wild Things Are*. London: Bodley Head.

17. Kerr, J. (1970) *Mog the Forgetful Cat*. London: Collins.

18. Barber, A. (1990) *The Mousehole Cat*. London: Walker Books.

19. Dahl, R. (1975) *Danny the Champion of the World*. London: Jonathan Cape Publishers.

20. Carter, D. (1999) *Misspellboobiland*. Mold: Clwyd Poetry Project.

21. Needle, J. (1978) *My Mate Shofiq*. London: André Deutsch Publishers.

22. Bawden, N. (1975) *Carrie's War*. London: Victor Gollancz.

23. Magorian, M. (1981) *Goodnight Mister Tom*. London: Kestrel Books.

Select bibliography

For the formulation of ideas

Auden, W. H. (1954) *Secondary Worlds*. London: Faber and Faber.

Bettelheim, B. (1976) *The Uses of Enchantment*. London: Thames and Hudson.

Bodkin, M. (1934) *Archetypal Patterns in Poetry*. London: Oxford University Press.

Brook, P. (1989) The 1989 *International Storytelling Festival Souvenir Programme*. London: The South Bank Centre.

Dewey, J. (1934) *Art as Experience*. New York: Minton, Balch and Company Publishers.

Finnegan, R. (1988) *Literacy and Orality*. London: Basil Blackwell Publishers.

Gadamer, H-G. (1986) *The Relevance of the Beautiful*. Cambridge: Cambridge University Press.

Goody, J. (1992) 'Oral culture' in Bauman, R. (ed.) *Folklore, Cultural Performances and Popular Entertainments*. London: Oxford University Press.

Harding, D. W. (1992) 'Psychological processes in the reading of fiction' in Meek, M. (ed.) *The Cool Web*. London: Bodley Head.

Havelock, E. (1986) *The Muse Learns to Write*. New Haven: Yale University Press.

Lord, A. B. (1960) *The Singer of Tales*. New York: Harvard University Press.

Neihardt, J. G. (1974) *Black Elk Speaks*. London: Abacus Paperbacks.

Ong, W. J. (1982) *Orality and Literacy*. London: Routledge.

Parry M. (1971) *The Making of Homeric Verse*. London: Oxford University Press.

Powling, C. (ed.) *Books for Keeps*. [magazine] London: Bodley Head.

Propp, V. (1982) *Theory and History of Folklore*. Manchester: Manchester University Press.

Shavit, Z. (1986) *Poetics of Children's Literature*. Athens, Georgia: University of Georgia Press.

Stannard, J. (1998) *The National Literacy Strategy Framework for teaching*, 5. London: Department for Education and Employment.

Watkins, T. and Sutherland, Z. (1995) 'Contemporary Children's Literature (1970-present)' in Hunt, P. (ed.) *Children's Literature, an illustrated history*. London: Oxford University Press.

Wells, G. (1986) The Meaning Makers. London: Hodder and Stoughton.

Winnicott, D. W. (1971) *Playing and Reality*, 12. London: Tavistock Publications.

Zipes, J. (1983) *Fairy Tales and the Art of Subversion*. London: Heinemann Books.

Editions used in literacy strategy lessons

Barber, A. *The Mousehole Cat*. Walker Books. ISBN: 0744523532.

Baum, L. F. *The Wizard of Oz*. Puffin Books. ISBN: 0140366938.

Bawden, N. *Carrie's War*. Puffin Books. ISBN: 0140306897.

Burnett. F. H. *The Secret Garden*. Puffin Books. ISBN: 0140366660.

Carter, D. *Misspellboobiland.* Clwyd Poetry Project at Pentre Farm, Woodhill, Oswestry, Shropshire. SY10 9AS.

Dahl, R. *Danny, the Champion of the World.* Puffin Books. ISBN: 0140371575.

Kerr, J. *Mog, the Forgetful Cat.* Harper Collins. ISBN: 0006640621.

Longfellow, H. W. *The Song of Hiawatha.* Everyman. ISBN: 0460872680.

Magorian, M. *Goodnight Mister Tom.* Puffin Books. ISBN: 0140372334.

Milne, A. A. *Pooh Invents a New Game.* Heinemann. ISBN: 0416171621.

Needle, J. *My Mate Shofiq.* Harper Collins. ISBN: 0006715184.

Sendak, M. *Where the Wild Things Are.* Harper Collins. ISBN: 0006640869.

Shakespeare, W. *The Tempest.* Penguin Books. ISBN: 0140707131.

Wilde, O. 'The Selfish Giant' in *The Happy Prince and Other Stories.* Puffin Books. ISBN: 0140503838

Tables

These tables offer to teachers and students a detailed planning summary of all the literacy strategy materials provided in Chapters 4, 5 and 6. These materials cover the fiction requirements in word, sentence and text level work for every term throughout the primary school from Reception to Year 6. Teachers and students of Key Stage 1 classes will need to supplement these materials, because the stories are short. However, the approaches are easily transferable from one book to another. Teachers and students of Key Stage 2 classes have a complete set of materials which should fully meet the fiction requirements of the Strategy.

The materials in Chapters 4, 5 and 6, however, go beyond the 'Framework for teaching'. Each set of lesson notes offers guidance on presentation of texts and activities in dance, drama, music and visual art. These activities are not intended as optional extras, but as integral to the whole experience of the work of literature, whether it be a short story such as Judith Kerr's 'Mog the Forgetful Cat' or a major work such as Shakespeare's *The Tempest*.

So, the tables below are intended as a means for teachers to check quickly what they will cover if they use the materials in this book.

- Table 1 summarises the range of work covered.
- Table 2 summarises the works of fiction used. The oral tradition stories include the name of the country from which the story comes.
- Table 3 summarises the literacy strategy objectives.
- Table 4 summarises work in the arts from the National Curriculum orders for English (drama), Art, Music and Physical Education (dance).

The best way of using these tables, therefore, is to come to them prior to planning fiction work for the half term, whole term or the year ahead and check off which objectives are included. Obviously, one work of literature cannot carry a comprehensive set of word and sentence level objectives. However, the majority of text level objectives are covered in the materials provided in Chapter 4, 5 and 6. Word and sentence level objectives not carried in these materials can either be taught separately or taught through the poetry and non-fiction ranges of work.

Table 1. Range of work statements

Year	Term One	Term Two	Term Three
Reception	Traditional story with predictable structure and patterned language.	Modern story with predictable structure and patterned language.	Traditional story with predictable structure and patterned language.
One	Story with familiar setting; predictable and repetitive pattern.	Story with familiar, predictable and patterned language from another culture.	Story about a fantasy world.
Two	Story with familiar setting.	Story from another culture.	Story by a significant children's author.
Three	Story with familiar setting.	Legend from a different culture.	Adventure story.
Four	Historical novel.	Novel about an imagined world.	Story that raises issues.
Five	Novel by a significant children's writer.	Legend from another culture.	Legend from another culture.
Six	Study of a Shakespeare play.	Longer established story from folk genre.	Comparison of two significant authors' treatments of the same theme.

Table 2. Works of fiction used

Year	Term One	Term Two	Term Three
Reception	*Why Monkeys Live in Trees*, Africa. **O**	*Where the Wild Things Are* by Maurice Sendak. **M**	*The Princess and the Pea* by Hans Andersen. **C**
One	*Mog the Forgetful Cat* by Judith Kerr. **M**	'The Nung Gwama', China. **O**	*Pooh Invents a New Game* by A. A. Milne. **C**
Two	*The Mousehole Cat* by Antonia Barber. **M**	'The Boy who Disappeared', Czech Republic. **O**	'The Selfish Giant' by Oscar Wilde. **C**
Three	*Danny the Champion of the World* by Roald Dahl. **M**	'The Blue Mountain', Norway. **O**	*The Wizard of Oz* by L. Frank Baum. **C**
Four	*The Secret Garden* by Frances Hodgson Burnett. **C**	*Misspellboobiland* by Dennis Carter. **M**	'The Wonderbird', Iran. **O**
Five	*My Mate Shofiq* by Jan Needle. **M**	*The Song of Hiawatha* by Henry Wadsworth Longfellow. **C**	'The Steel Monster', Armenia. **O**
Six	*The Tempest* by William Shakespeare. **C**	'The Soldier's Fiddle', Russia. **O**	*Carrie's War* by Nina Bawden & *Goodnight Mister Tom* by Michelle Magorian. **M**

O Story from the oral tradition.
C Story from the classical inheritance.
M Story from modern children's fiction.

Table 3. Learning objectives covered

Year	Term One	Term Two	Term Three
Reception	Word 2,3,5,7,9. Sentence 1,2,3,4. Text: Reading 2,3,4,6,7,8. Text: Writing 11.	Word 2,5,7,9,10. Sentence 1,2,3. Text: Reading 2,3,4,5,6,7,8. Text: Writing 12.	Word 5,7,9,10,11. Sentence 1,2,3. Text: Reading 1,2,4. Text: Writing 14
One	Word 4,5,6. Sentence 4. Text: Reading 1,3,4,5,7. Text: Writing 9,11.	Word 2,3. Sentence 4,5,7. Text: Reading 1,4,5,8,9,10,11. Text: Writing 6,7,8,9.	Word 1,8. Sentence 1,3. Text: Reading 3,5,6,10. Text: Writing 13,14.
Two	Word 3,4,7,8,10. Sentence 1,5. Text: Reading 1,3,4,5,6. Text: Writing 9,11.	Word 2,3,4,5,11. Sentence 2,6,7,8. Text: Reading 2,4,5,6,7. Text: Writing 13,14 .	Word 1,6,9. Sentence 1,6. Text: Reading 3,4,5,7. Text: Writing 10.
Three	Word 1,4. Sentence 1,2,3,4,5,6,7,8. Text: Reading 1,2,3,4,5. Text: Writing 10,14.	Word 1,2,4,18,19,24. Sentence 2,3,4,5,6,7. Text: Reading 1,2,3. Text: Writing 6,7,8,9.	Word 1,2. Sentence 1,2,6. Text: Reading 1,2,3,4,5,9 Text: Writing 10,12,13.
Four	Word 1,9,11. Sentence 2,3. Text: Reading 1,2,3,4,5,6. Text: Writing 9,10,11,12,13.	Word 1. Sentence 1,2. Text: Reading 1,2,3,4. Text: Writing 10,12,13.	Word 1,5. Sentence 2. Text: Reading 1,2,3. Text: Writing 11,12,13.
Five	Word 8,9. Sentence 5,6,7,8. Text: Reading 1,3,9,10. Text: Writing 13,18,19.	Word 4,11. Sentence 5,9,10. Text: Reading 1,3,4,5,8,10. Text: Writing 11,12,13.	Word 1,2,3,11,12. Sentence 3. Text: Reading 1,4. Text: Writing 7,8,10.
Six	Word 7,10. Sentence – Text: Reading 1,2,3,5. Text: Writing 6,7,8,9.	Word 3,5. Sentence 1,5. Text: Reading 1,8. Text: Writing 10,11,12,14	Word – Sentence 2. Text: Reading 1,6. Text: Writing 10,11,12,14.

Table 4. Coverage of the arts in the National Curriculum

All references to 'Programmes of Study' in *Key Stages 1 and 2 of the National Curriculum.*

Year	Term One	Term Two	Term Three
Reception	*Art* U1/M1,3/I1. *Dance* 3a,c. *Drama* SL1d. *Music* –	*Art* U1/M1,3/I2. *Dance* 3a,c. *Drama* SL1d. *Music* P2/C1,2/A1.	*Art* M3/I2. *Dance* 3a,b. *Drama* SL1d. *Music* –
One	*Art* U1/M1/I2. *Dance* 3a,c. *Drama* SL1d. *Music* P2,4/C1,2/A1,2.	*Art* M1/I1. *Dance* 3a,c. *Drama* SL1d. *Music* P2.	*Art* M1,3/I2. *Dance* 3a,b. *Drama* SL1d. *Music* P2,3,4,5,6,7/ C2,4,5/A1.
Two	*Art* U1/M1,3/I2. *Dance* 3a,c. *Drama* SL1d. *Music* P3,4,5,6,7/ C2,3,4,5/A4.	*Art* U1/M1,3/I1. *Dance* 3a,c. *Drama* SL1d. *Music* P2,4,5,6,7/ C1,2,3,4,5/A1	*Art* U1,3/M1,3/I2. *Dance* 3a,b *Drama* SL1d. *Music* P4,4,6,7/C2,4,5/ A1,3,4.
Three	*Art* U1/M1,3/I2,4. *Dance* – *Drama* SL1d. *Music* P4,5,6,7/ C2,3,5/A1,4,5.	*Art* U1/M1,3/I2,4. *Dance* 3a,c. *Drama* SL1d. *Music* P2,4,5,6,7/ C1,2,3,4,5/A1,5.	*Art* U1/M1,2,3/I2,4,5. *Dance* 3a,b. *Drama* SL1d. *Music* P2,3,4,5,6,7/ C1,2,3,4,5/A1,3,4,5.
Four	*Art* U1/M1,2,3/I2,3. *Dance* – *Drama* SL1d. *Music* P4,5,6,7/ C1,2,3,4,5/A4,5.	*Art* U1/M1,3/I2,4. *Dance* 3a,c. *Drama* SL1d. *Music* P3,4,5,6,7/ C2,3,4,5/A1,5.	*Art* U1/M1,3/I2,4. *Dance* 3a,c. *Drama* SL1d. *Music* P2,4,5,6,7/ C1,2,3,4,5/A1,3,4,5.
Five	*Art* U1/M1,3/I2,4. *Dance* – *Drama* SL1d. *Music* P4,5,6,7/C2,3,4,5/ A4,5.	*Art* U1,3/M1,2,3/I2,4. *Dance* 3a,b. *Drama* SL1d. *Music* P4,5,6,7/C2,3,4,5/ A3,4,5.	*Art* U1/M1,2,3/I2,4. *Dance* – *Drama* SL1d. *Music* P5,6,7/C1,2,3,4,5/ A1,3,4,5.
Six	*Art* U1,3/M1,3/I2,4. *Dance* 3a,b. *Drama* SL1d. *Music* P3,4,5,6,7/ C2,3,4,5/A3,4,5.	*Art* U1/M3/I2,4. *Dance* – *Drama* SL1d. *Music* P5,6,7/C2,4,5/ A4,5.	*Art* U1/M1,3/I2,4. *Dance* 3a,c. *Drama* SL1d. *Music* P4,5,6,7/C2,5/ A4,5.

KEY.

Art.
U: Understanding. M: Making. I: Investigating.

Dance (P.E.)
3: Dance.

Drama (English).
SL: Speaking and listening.

Music.
P: Playing. C: Composing. A: Appraising.

Index

Printed in the United Kingdom
by Lightning Source UK Ltd.
104962UKS00002B/111-118